She called me TETCHED

GUS STEFANOW

Published by GUS STEFANOW, 2024.

SHE CALLED ME TETCHED

First edition. April 2, 2024.

Copyright © 2024 GUS STEFANOW.

ISBN: 979-8224279319

Written by GUS STEFANOW.

Table of Contents

1909 | Chapter 1 1

Roaring Twenties | Chapter 2 7

Depression Survival | Chapter 3.. 17

World War Two | Chapter 4... 25

Beautiful Ohio I | Chapter 5 33

The Willie Wars | Chapter 6 43

Independents Days | Chapter 7 51

Kentucky for the win | Chapter 8 65

Smallwood kennel and farms Chapter 9... 79

Post Papaw Kentucky | Chapter 10 91

Hangin' on, Honey! | Chapter 11 99

Beautiful Ohio II | Chapter 12...109

Beulah Land | Chapter 13 119

Grandmother. Lunatic. Merciless. Formidable. Jemima Smallwood fit many descriptions. This book highlights close to one hundred years of life for my maternal grandmother. Her zest for life was only exceeded by her orneriness and downright meanness. Her stories are forever entrenched in family lore and are worthy of telling. An enigma as a larger-than-life personality, she taught her offspring well. She was profane, *hilarious*, and brutal. "She called me *TETCHED*" is her story and a description put on me. Read if you dare.

Gus Stefanow

1909

Chapter 1

The United States grew into a fledgling superpower in the early 1900s. The Industrial Age ushered in mass production of anything one could imagine. Goods flew out of factories, working personnel to max capacity six days per week, year in and year out. Life expectancy for Americans born in 1909 stood at age 50.5 overall. Jemima's long life nearly doubled that, by the grace of God. Air travel expanded in its infancy across the country. Admiral Perry reached the North Pole on his sixth try.

Meanwhile, in rural southeastern Kentucky, an expanding family got a new baby girl they named Jemima. Although uncommon, it represented the name of the Biblical Job's second daughter after the trials he endured. It seems a more fitting name now amongst the family when one considers the difficulties of the woman many learned to call "Mamaw" over her chaotic, violent life. She hated her legal name all her days. She preferred Jaybird, Jay, or Bunt instead.

One of five children born to Franklin and Emily Smith, she chased siblings John (Also known as Hoss), William (Dick), and Eva (Ev) as soon as she could walk. She said she was born in a log cabin like old Abe Lincoln, but nobody verified it. Never to be outdone by man or beast, her tomboy ways started in her from the get-go. Later, she chased her little sister, Ada (Odie or Ode), her lifetime partner-in-crime!

Jemima became a defiant child at a youthful age. She could not be swayed easily by anyone or anything. Put her up at the gates of Hell, and she'd spit on the rails, daring the Prince of Darkness to get her. A strong-willed spitfire, her attitude guided her pursuit of happiness with the sharpness of a heat-seeking missile. Intimidation? It must have been for others because Jemima feared *nothing*.

Farm life continued, pausing briefly for World War One. Most folks in the Kentucky hills saw it as an annoyance more than anything. Some brethren served in the Great War, as named. Many returned to coal-mining jobs and equated them to the trench warfare they'd survived. Life proved challenging for this crowd.

Jemima never mentioned much of her early years to any of us, her offspring. Were there things she didn't want us to know? One glance from her accusing eyes silenced most inquiries, including mine. She peered deep into one's soul to make mere mortals uncomfortable. That discomfort kept us from prying any further. What little we do know has to come forward to properly honor a woman a light-year ahead of her peers if any such peers existed.

The woman grew up fearless from birth. Farm living required the physical stamina of men, or so conventional wisdom of the times advocated. With just two sons and three daughters, the Smith clan took an alternate route. Their girls were treated as males, like it or not! No pretty playthings, dolls, or anything feminine were allowed because they only took away from the independent mindset the family lived by.

Jemima loved her family's team of horses. While her older brothers insisted she cleaned stalls because of her age and gender, Jemima also groomed and exercised them regularly. Considering her youth and inexperience, her brothers were alarmed at how fast she'd ride, but Pa let her do it her way. She supplied the horses with plenty of drinking water while inspecting bridles and saddles. Her rapport with the magnificent beasts was better than with any humans, with Pa and Ma being notable exceptions. Animals became her trademark interest, and she loved every one of them. People, not so much!

Chores before sunrise occurred daily. Animals needed tending to, hay needed baling, and crops required attention and added to the grind of farm life. Everyone worked because everyone wanted to eat. If anyone slacked off, the whole family suffered. Survival for all only happened when all pulled their weight. Slackers were dealt with immediately and harshly.

What today's language calls a "side hustle" began for the Smith family in earnest before World War One and continued into the 1950s. Farming dealt with harsh weather, insects, drought, and fluctuating prices. Illegal liquor filled a void that regular farming could not. A perfect pick-me-up when needed but also medicinal. Its revenue stream came in handy, particularly in winter months.

Ma Smith stood adamantly opposed to alcohol. A tonic for the sick, it took away many folks by its charms when overdone. She showed nothing but contempt for its existence. A devout Christian, she allowed no single drop to be stored in her home. That said, she did learn to cap the concoction Pa made in the barn, smokehouse, henhouse, or root cellar to keep the law from finding out. With each batch, she wore a scarf over her face because of the "demon rum"; she could not tolerate the smell. With starvation a threat, she compromised on liquor to see her children grow.

Pa Smith kept an open mind about liquor. His love of the sacred Scriptures and devotion to his faith made him realize that if Jesus turned water into wine, then, indeed, humanity benefitted from it. The only restrictions he saw came in the drunkenness, not the imbibing itself. The apostle Paul said, "To take a little wine for frequent stomach ailments." If the most prolific writer of the New Testament said it, then Pa approved its production. The United States government and the State of Kentucky begged to differ, but the Smith clan were survivors. These were the laws of men and not God. Hallelujah, some might say.

Keeping the secret recipe just proved more demanding than the family realized. Snooping eyes came around, wondering how the family got along in lean times. There were always tough times in this part of the state. One day, a sheriff came by on what today might be called a wellness visit. The Smith family believed that snitches got stitches but went along with the lawman's ruse.

"Frank, we care so much about the county's citizens that we sometimes check on 'em unannounced. Doin' our Christian duty, you might say! The 'pox goes round up in these here mountains, just like tuberculosis and such, so since we ain't got many doctors 'round here, well, they send me for a look-see, you know?" the sheriff said.

"Oh yeah, I understand that Harley, I do. Remember when the government started that draft and come 'round for our boys up here? Well, I don't recall you bein' here then! Christian duties is it now, huh?" Pa asked.

"Well, now, Frank, I know there ain't no dummies up in these parts with your kin! You know, anybody who'd try cheatin' Uncle Sam out of liquor money. Not one soul should even try." The sheriff answered.

"All I know is folks here just wanna be left alone. We pursue our own happiness and don't give a hoot in Hell for anyone tryin' to interfere. You get what I mean, Harley?" Pa spouted out.

The conversation got tense in a hurry. The sheriff stopped beating around the bush and produced the real reason for the visit.

"Frank, the word is someone out this way is makin', bottlin', and sellin' moonshine! Now you know I got my duties, bein' the peace officer in this county! I don't want no trouble, but...can I take a quick gander in the house? I mean, the state bureau boys are comin' down hard on this stuff!"

"Sure, now Harley, we go back a far piece in our lives. I know you got your job, but I promise you'll find nothin' illegal here! We're God-fearin', Bible-totin' Christian people. You do what you must!" Pa replied.

The sheriff sheepishly walked into the house as Ma prepared the evening meal. Her eyes glared a hole through the man, causing grief this day. She nodded and went back to breading the chicken for dinner.

The man made his rounds and found nothing to alarm him. Little Jemima feigned sniffles and lay in bed with a bogus fever. The sheriff warned of something goin' round every season that could take people out. He quietly said goodbye, got back on his horse, and disappeared. His detection skills could have been better, but the man performed as required.

"Okay, Bunt, you can get up now! He's gone down the road and outta sight!" Ma yelled to her fourth of five children.

"Lord mercy, mommy, I thought that man would sit down on my bed! *Then* what would I have said, huh? I stayed still and played it up. Do you reckon they take ten-year-old girls to big people jail? I sure wouldn't want to be without my family!" Jemima asked innocently.

The family erupted with laughter, not so much as what Jemima said but how she meant it. How might she have explained the liquor jars under her pillow, blankets, and headboard? Pa chuckled and explained.

"Little woman, Harley has a duty to find stills, moonshine, and such every once in a while. He's no fool, but this is his way of warnin' us. We gotta be careful with what we make for our kin! The truth is he knew not to sit on that bed! Now we gotta move that 'shine so's yer Ma don't get riled up with it inside. You done a respectable job actin' sick, so you get the first piece of chicken for dinner tonight!"

The victory dinner made Pa feel like celebrating a little more than usual. His stash of 'shine sat under a loose board in the barn wall. After a great meal, dessert was an after-dinner swallow of "the great skull cracker." Pa felt so good after one that it led to two, and then...

Pa wandered out into the street, dancing and singing pieces of old hymns and Irish bar tunes. He went towards the town and was nearly run over multiple times by wagonloads of townsfolk, laughing at Pa's overindulgence.

Ma noticed how long he'd been gone. She wandered the property, screeching his name as she went. Without luck, she investigated the barn and went straight to Pa's stash of the hard stuff.

"Durn him! Durn him all to Hell and back!" Ma said under her breath so the children didn't hear.

Ma rounded up the kids and sent them in different directions to find their lost father. She stewed; her face red as the sun as they took off. The boys took horses while Eva and Jemima went off on foot.

"Ev, what we gonna do if we find Pa? What if he's hurt or somethin'?" Jemima questioned.

Ev, or Eva, became Jemima's confidante and older sister by more than seven years. She'd grown into a wise-cracking, stoic young lady wise beyond her age.

"Jaybird, you worry too damn much! And if you say I swore, know I will haunt your dreams, little lady, every night! Pa's got himself a snootful of the 'shine, and he's prolly in a ditch someplace!" Eva said.

The girls walked on and hoped they'd find their father before their know-it-all brothers. Indeed, Ma paid a nice bounty to the kids bringing Daddy home. Time passed, but the sisters heard faint singing over a ridge.

"Oh, Danny boy...uh...the pipes, the pies, hahaha, the pipers are callin', fallin' down the mountainside! Hahaha! Oh, shall we gather at the river, the river, the river, Hehehehehe, that ol' man river! 'Cuz, she'll be comin' round the mountain when she comes, my Emily will be comin' round that mountain, hahaha!" Pa slurred, getting louder as the girls closed in. His revelry made him unaware his girls heard him so clearly.

"Daddy, uh, you're drunk, and Ma sent us to fetch you!" Eva said sternly.

The man returned to singing, not caring that his children were there. Eva saw this behavior several times, but not young Jemima.

"Eva, sister, he don't even know it's us! He's plain blind by that stuff he drunk! Ma is gonna skin him alive! I'm feared for his soul when he gets home, Eva!" Jemima squealed.

Eva witnessed enough. Their father stumbled and sang as they tried to steer him towards home. A lean, muscular farmer, Pa displayed the build of a welterweight boxer and fists to match.

"Who you two be? Huh? Why I'm just lettin' off a lil built up steam, young'uns! Your mommy sent you for me, didn't she? Well, you can tell her I am a full-growed man! A man with his own brain to think and think on things! You two are my young'uns, you say, right?" Pa asked.

Eva didn't bother to answer the questions anymore. Her patience measured in nanoseconds when the Good Lord produced her. She let go of her father as he leaned on Jemima momentarily. Once Eva latched back on, she didn't let go.

Eva pulled out a knife she kept hidden in her dress as a "just in case" some ignorant male tried anything with her. She cut off a hickory limb, ran her hands down it to remove the leaves, and then beat the backs of her drunken father's legs!

"Move, old man, I say, move! Durn your hide and the liquor you swilled down. Move, move I say!" Eva commanded.

"Hey now, you don't hit your pappy this way, you young'un's! I'll get home on my own!" Pa protested as Jemima struggled to keep up with him.

"No, you won't, Daddy. You gonna keep goin' the direction me and Jaybird send you. It'll be dark soon, and we ain't gonna be out amongst the old haints! (Translation- ghost) We *know* them woods!" Eva insisted.

Pa complied, and his singing died out as he hustled, stumbling. He'd face the music soon enough when Emily, his wife, met him at the door. The kids scattered, and the horses were put away in their stalls for the night.

Ma did not intend to argue with a drunken male who'd surely forget the conversation by morning. She kept a close eye on her man, even telling him she'd found his hiding place. A new, more prosperous America awaited just around the corner, but how might southeastern Kentucky see it? The Smith clan roared into the 1920s.

Roaring Twenties
Chapter 2

With the short-term war behind them, the Smith clan and everyone else concentrated on the good life and prosperity of the 1920s. What that looked like was anyone's guess because so many newfangled inventions seemed like science fiction to families scraping by year in, year out.

Life mostly stayed the same in rural Kentucky in the Roaring Twenties. Life went on as it had for the decades beforehand. Coal mining and farming were the twin towers of society. A few lucky folks had radios, but most did not for decades. Outside-world access came through travel or printed media only.

Jemima became the consummate athletic child. No boy bested her in any physical contest, especially her smart-aleck brothers. She grew tall and ran swiftly over the hills of Kentucky. Fear? She showed zero tolerance for it! If that old emotion took hold, she quickly stomped and killed it altogether. The spirit of self-reliance rose in her from her first breath. She may have been born with chainmail as her superpower.

Throughout Jemima's lifetime, she consistently spoke of the supernatural as others might talk about the weather or politics. She told everyone that some folks are born with the gift of being sensitive to spiritual/mystical realms. Not merely conjecture or speculation but part of the facts passed between generations. Witches, ghouls, and goons of all varieties walked "amongst 'em" in every holler in America, especially in Appalachia.

Ma and Pa Smith's growing family needed more space. With the birth of their youngest daughter Odie years beforehand, a local farm came up for sale, so they made an offer. A few weeks later, after negotiations and counteroffers, the deal came through. The dream came to fruition, and the family celebration took hold. Unfortunately, the cheer didn't last for the Smith clan.

Rumors flew through the county that one person, none-too-pleased about losing the sale of her dream home, simmered. The female proprietor of a local general store carried herself in Mafia fashion. Her words were law, and she didn't take the undercutting of real estate kindly. She breathed threats of retribution in certain circles, promising to exact revenge. Even in bright sunlight, the darkness around her made folks believe she dabbled in the black arts. One wild Christian with a temper didn't back down. Guess who? Yes, Jemima!

The Smiths settled into the new farm with extraordinary optimism accompanying a victory over fellow suitors for a nice piece of ground. The fields surrounding the home were picture-perfect. Wells and streams provided fresh water for everyone, including livestock and fields. Multiple barns gave shelter to animals, wagons, and the tools required for such an operation.

A day came when Ma Smith needed a few supplies from the general store nearby. Nearby is a relative term, as in several miles away. She made a compact list, handed Jemima the money, and told her to hurry. When Odie begged to go too, Ma Smith agreed if the two could stay out of trouble. The two sisters were known county-wide for mischief, a fact that persistently dogged them throughout their long lifetimes.

The two pre-teens left for the store on a sunny, southeastern Kentucky day. They passed no neighbors as they slogged along, picking at each other for liking boys from the same family at church. The carefree day took a dark turn as the store came into view.

With few resources for commerce in the area, the shopping situation proved woefully inadequate for the community. The general store gave all or nothing to everyone. Jemima and Odie walked into a hornet's nest.

The girls pushed open the screen door with enthusiasm as they arrived. People looked around at them as they entered, as many were prone to do. Jemima noticed the nicely kept, well-swept store, but an upstanding broom in the corner sent chills down her spine. She took Odie by the hand, and they trotted back outside, scurrying away from nosy patrons.

"Ode, Ode, I swear, that old woman in there must be a witch! My Lord, I believe it! I saw that broom standin' on its end and it's for shore a sign!" Jemima said in excitement.

Less convinced, Odie became bug-eyed with fear at the forefront of her mind. She shook as she spoke.

"Bunt, are you for sure she's a witch, I mean a real one? Mommy gave us this money for these supplies here so we gotta get 'em!"

Jemima gathered her thoughts and plan. She told Odie neither should make direct eye contact so the woman couldn't steal their souls! They set about to get in and out quickly. They didn't want suspicions revealed that they held deep inside themselves.

Jemima opened the screen door again, looking around for the few items needed. Odie stuck like glue to Jemima's side while she stared at the floor, ceiling, or anything but the proprietor.

The old woman popped out from behind a display and scared the bejesus out of both! Jemima let out a war whoop as Odie ran in place, unable to breathe! Both collided with one another to run away. Other store shoppers laughed their heads off. The old woman and the girls did not find it funny.

"What do you young'uns want in here, huh? I come around the corner to help you and you look like you seen a ghost, I say!" the old lady bellowed.

Odie held out the list and shook like Don Knotts as she handed it over to the woman. Jemima stood erect, faced the woman with the quizzical look she'd become known for, and spoke out.

"Our mother sent us here to get these supplies and git back home before the day is gone! We just moved into our farm, and there's much work waitin'!"

The old woman's face turned an ashy grey; her slight smile turned itself upside down as if she'd imbibed in a vinegar-and-lemon juice cocktail. She stepped towards the girls militantly and spoke up.

"Well, well. You people stole my farm did you? I ain't ever gonna forget it! I placed that farm in my sights for years and just knew it as mine! So, you think you're gonna enjoy it there, huh? You better think again! You tell your folks I said so and when I promise something, believe you me, it comes to pass. You'll never get a minutes peace so long as you live in that stolen house!"

Odie slyly took the list back from the old woman's hand and searched for each item required. Jemima stood toe to toe with the old woman and made threats of her own.

"Look, my folks bought that farm fair and square! We needed the room, so we'll work the land and prosper. We Smith's don't do well with threats from anyone! We don't back down, you hear me?" Jemima replied with volume.

Odie gathered everything needed and nudged Jemima for the money Ma gave her. The lady looked at them with disgust but rang up the purchases, bagged them, and gave the correct change. War drums hummed.

"You young'uns be sure to tell your folks what I said, you hear me? No peace long as you live there. And you'll both see a sign and a wonder on your way home. I guarantee it!" He-he-he, she laughed as the girls made their way to the door. Jemima could not resist one last zinger.

"Listen here, you old bitch, you lost the farm since you bid too durn low, hear me? Ya don't wanna mess with us because you're not prepared for my family! No, no old haint gonna run us off! You got that? Don't make us come for you, because if you do, why, there won't be a piece of you left!"

The other patrons bristled at Jemima's language and promised to tell her folks. The old lady chuckled as the girls took off with a spring in their steps.

The girls only conversed once they were several hundred yards away and out of sight. Fear continued to make Odie uncomfortable and irritated at her big, unrepentant sister.

"Bunt, uh, did you have to talk like that to her? I mean, gee, if she is a witch, you gonna be the first to go! And I don't wanna have a life without you! It just don't make sense, you, and that mouth of yours. You don't even try to hush it much!"

Jemima appreciated the sentiment but felt irritated that her little sister questioned her defense of the Smith name.

"That ol' witch ain't gonna do nothing we can't manage, Ode! I'm tellin' you, she ain't gonna run us off, got it? And don't you go tellin' the folks when we get home, you hear?"

Odie knew the wrath of her older, wiser, and meaner sister. She shook mightily in her shoes as she brooded over a response. She replied to Jemima.

"But you're gonna have your way no matter what I say; that much I know! I'll stay quiet just as long as I can, but..."

Jemima couldn't wait to interject. The silence demanded an answer.

"Now, now you're worryin' too much, like you always do, my dear sister. Everything will work, you'll see."

The peaceful walk continued until rustling happened in the bushes. Both girls stopped to see the commotion. They stood silently and stared into the brush.

Suddenly, a rooster appeared and flew directly overhead! It came at the girls, diving as a prehistoric pterodactyl, screeching and diving as they ran enthusiastically toward the house. In a strange show of strength, the rooster stayed overhead for hundreds of yards before trailing into the forest.

The frightened girls dove under a tree to catch their breath and surveyed the surroundings. Breathing heavily, Odie spoke first.

"Now are you gonna tell Ma and Pa about the ol' witch or not? Lord have mercy, Bunt, that's no ordinary rooster! That thing is the *devil*! Did you see how that animal acted?"

Jemima didn't try to disagree about the fowl, making them flee. Did the prophecy come true? It seemed that way.

"Jesus, Ode, I am glad you kept up when I turned on my top speed! Lord, I didn't know which way to turn! I still say we keep quiet for as long as we can. We're *even* now with the ol' witch, right? She done scared us, so maybe we done with her ass!" Jemima muttered.

Odie was terrified and agreed. They quickly moved on the road, eyeing the sky for the monster that frightened them. The farm came into view, and both felt like they'd crossed into a safe zone.

Neither girl mentioned the things she had seen and experienced. It did not take long before the peace of the new farm came under attack.

The Smith children went to bed one night after the family dinner and an evening of stories and jokes. Ma and Pa sat with the coal-oil lights on for a few moments of quiet in their custom. Bed awaited, nighttime prayers, and then off to dreamland.

Just as the couple headed to the bedroom, a knock came from the front door. The family dogs barked as Pa went to answer and found nobody there when he opened. Unfazed, he shrugged and decided his imagination got the best of him.

Back in the bedroom, the couple heard a knock again at the front door. Pa got up and went to the door with a little irritated swing to his steps. If a joke were being played, nobody laughed.

The results were the same. No soul at the door, on the porch, or anywhere to be seen. Pa sighed loudly and walked back across the floor to the bedroom. Ma saw concern and irritation on the man's face.

"Honey, what in tarnation is goin' on out there? Someone's playin' a joke, I reckon. Are we all gonna get up and search out the trouble?" Ma asked.

"No, I don't reckon that's necessary just yet. I just can't figure how they get away from eyesight when I'm so close. It's a moonlit night so I can see good out there!" Pa answered.

By the next go-round, Pa heard enough. He loaded his shotgun with buckshot and prepared to at least lay a round or two into the night sky to scare off the troublemaker! When he went to the door, again, no one was there. He walked outside, shotgun in one hand and lamp in the other. He went around the house perimeter and saw nothing unusual.

Ma met him at the front door this time. She was irritated and afraid that the kids could remain sleepless. The children gathered in the living room to assess the situation to nobody's surprise. Pa took the lead in the conference.

"Oh, you children don't need to worry none. Somebody's out there playin' a game! When I catch 'em, he won't be tormentin' anyone!"

Ma shooed everyone back to their bunks, but at least two offspring suspected the obvious. Two sisters talked in hushed tones while Pa sat in his rocking chair, shotgun atop his lap.

"Bunt, Bunt...we gotta tell 'em what's happenin'! I say we take our medicine now, then we get together and beat that witch to pieces!" Odie whispered. Jemima listened but told her to go to sleep.

Pa nearly fell asleep in his chair when the next knock came. He stumbled to his feet, opened the door quickly, and no soul appeared. Pa fumed!

Pa walked into the cool night air and fired two rounds from his favorite weapon, one at a time. The loud booms silenced the dogs but provided the opposite effect on his clan. They all gathered, madder than wet hens, to offer anything for peace. They'd reached a breaking point.

"Everybody, listen to me. Y'all get dressed since it appears nary a one of us is gonna get any sleep tonight. We'll find who's doin' this, I guarantee it!" Pa said.

Everyone threw on their clothes and prepared for battle. Pa looked around the room and told them all to wait. The tormentor's return seemed imminent.

It wasn't long before knocking began again. Pa rushed out the door as some followed him while others took to the back entrance. The commotion stirred up the dogs and anyone or anything in earshot! To everyone's amazement, nobody saw a sign of anyone. The family searched the farm's perimeter and found nothing to lead them to believe a visitor had come by.

Once inside again, Odie pulled Jemima aside for counsel. The confession must come out, and soon!

"Bunt, Bunt, we gotta tell 'em what's goin' on! Ain't nobody gonna get an ounce of sleep and we know why! Sissy, please jest let 'em know!" Odie whispered.

Jemima knew that a confession came before swift punishment and didn't relish the idea. "Spare the rod, spoil the child" stayed in vogue for centuries with no hope of changing overnight. Jemima whispered a warning to Odie.

"Ode, I guarantee we'll get a lickin' we'll never forget, now. How are we gonna tell everybody what I done without that? You gonna get a hand slap compared to what Pa will do to me! You ain't thinkin' straight!"

The knocking started with the clan huddled in the house again, to nobody's surprise. At first, they seethed and tried to ignore it. Pa cursed the darkness outside.

"I don't know who you are, but when I get my hands on you, there won't be a piece of you left! You hear me?" Pa screamed.

Jemima and Odie glared at each other with daring eyes. Neither could tell the folks now that Pa's anger was boiling. The Smith clan got zero sleep that night.

The family adjusted to their new surroundings as everyone does, and no one mentioned the calamity that caused such a stir. Deep in their minds, they thought the madness might all just go away, but it bubbled under the surface of everyday living.

New nosy neighbors dropped by one day to present an early version of a welcome wagon. A half dozen of the most curious came hat in hand to see how the clan adapted. Everyone made small talk, gave their approval, and then said their goodbyes. All that is, except one.

An enthusiastic woman named Bond took her time going out the door with the crowd. Her eyes detailed every change in the interior and the landscaping like a well-placed spy with reconnaissance duties. That zeal for detail got her noticed by Ma and Pa Smith as she exited.

"Eh, young woman, are you lookin' for somethin' round here?" Pa asked shyly.

"Well, yes sir, I am lookin' at what my home's gonna be when I get it. You see, you people stole it from under my mama and it don't set well with her! She won't rest and neither will you until she gets to be the rightful owner!" Bond replied smugly.

Ma spoke up before Pa did, and not in a charitable way.

"Looky here, little woman, we got this farm fair and square, we did! You can squirm and scream, do what you gotta, but this is *Smith* property! Get along now before I make you! I am not a violent woman, for sure, but you making my blood boil!"

The twenty-something busybody grinned and nodded as she waved goodbye. She stood at the edge of the property and waved her arms in a strange maneuver while shimmering snake-like. Pa restrained Ma because he knew things were getting out of control.

The couple locked their front door in an unusual act for them in the country. The timely conversations that followed made the pair wonder if the strange occurrences were because of the woman they unknowingly let into their home. The Smiths gathered their intelligence information.

A mere matter of days later, the knocking at night commenced again. The family knew another long night awaited. When hours passed without sleep, tempers flared, and the entire clan searched the property outside only to come up empty. Pa stopped at the front door to inventory his kin.

"All right, all right! We are all here now. I don't know what to make of it, but tomorrow I am gettin' the sheriff out here! This must stop!"

A loud thud came from the living room before he turned the knob to go inside. Pa stopped in his tracks as another deafening thud happened. He looked around, then spoke.

"Y'all hear that, young'un's? Hush! Just listen!"

Boom...bang... crash came knocking from inside the home. The frightened family looked in horror at the house, some unable to move. Ma pushed through the crowd with Jemima to her side, showing instant bravery.

"I don't know what or who you are but get outta my house!" Ma yelled.

The army of Smiths followed inside closely, making that impossible to tell where one soul began and another ended. Pa went for his family Bible while Ma prayed for strength to endure the night. Soon, the knocking started back up, but outside again.

Pa read from his Bible while Ma silently prayed with the kids. Sensing a tough spiritual battle, the crew dug deep into their faith. It needed to stretch a little more than they anticipated. The silence returned for a while, but everyone knew the war could resume anytime.

Pa convinced the county sheriff and a deputy to visit at sundown a few days later. Neither man could do anything more than run down a troublemaker with a penchant for mischief. Reluctantly, they kept their promise and moved inside the home.

For hours, nothing happened to upset the sheriff's foolproof plan. With everyone participating, they'd fan out, surround the house, and catch the instigator. Half the group scampered out the front door while the rest ventured between home and the barn. The simple plan went into action.

Most of the crowd sat in silence as Ma prayed. The knock came soon after, and everyone sprinted to their positions outside. Again, they found no one. The sheriff gathered the crew together in front of the house and started to speak in amazement when Pa heard the pounding inside again.

"Listen, listen y'all! Hush. It's inside the durn house!" Pa said in low tones.

Without hesitation, both sheriffs ran into the house with weapons drawn, sure the culprit stood inside. A complete sweep came up empty. The sheriff sadly spoke and addressed everyone.

"People, unless this here person can fly or walk through walls, we got nothing to go on! I ain't seen nothing like this in my life. We'll come back if you want us to, but I have no answers as to what's plaguing you all."

The family kindly thanked the men and let them leave. Pa's response to everyone dealing with the supernatural meant that the church people needed to act. He set about stopping in any church to tell his story. Days went by before a contingency of Baptists, Pentecostals, and Holiness-types showed up to pray over the farm.

Word spread that something odd went on at the farm. Some came by to look at the location. Others said the family made the story up for publicity's sake. The bravest souls who came to rid the presence got their money's worth.

People became comfortable as pastors and laypeople joined forces to exorcise the home and surrounding grounds. Reading scripture passages about protection and power gave a palpable sense of calm. Only two youngsters knew the source of the problem and were not telling anyone.

The Smith clan settled into routines typical of farm living. The relief let the family put their guard down. It was only natural after the ordeal, yet it became a catalyst for serious action.

Late one night, the knocking began again. The dogs went crazy, and the house shook with the activity of a large, frightened family. The chaos angered some, while others decided the cursed farm had to go. Were the witch rumors a reality? Pa made a command decision without delay.

"Everybody hold on now! Don't nobody do anything, okay? There's gotta be some explanation, but we ain't waitin' on it! We used the law and the Lord here, but whatever we dealin' with just don't give up easily! Get dressed, you all! We movin' somewhere! We'll stay up 'til sunrise and pack- then we go! I have seen and heard plenty!"

Were they running in victory or retreating to live to fight another day? Ma agreed with Pa that the place wasn't worth the torment and terror. By daybreak, the clan packed what they cared to take and left expeditiously. Kinfolk took the sojourners in while Ma and Pa sought out new housing. No one dared look back for fear of ending up like the biblical Lot's wife!

The field of candidates to own the Smith farm displayed a minuscule group. No one even wanted to look inside it. Weeks after the departure, the farm and outbuildings mysteriously burned. How that happened stays speculation. Jemima and sister Odie held their information within and took it to their graves with a hint of gasoline scent. Neither woman gave any assumption about the property's fate. Still, Jemima kept a satisfied look that people did not question. Nobody pushed a Smith around!

Depression Survival

Chapter 3

The feel-good times for America ended on a terrible October day in 1929. Coast-to-coast anxiety and fear swept through the landscape, and even the hollers of Kentucky were not spared. The calamity touched every part of American life.

Jemima met a handsome man named Johnie Brummett, and the courtship culminated in marriage on March 24, 1930. Johnie was a hardworking country boy who loved Jemima to the moon and back. With the world's cares on their shoulders, the newlyweds carved out an existence sometimes known as living.

Soon after the knot-tying, news came of a blessed event coming due in January 1931- a baby! Ma and Pa Smith rejoiced as the kinfolk did what they could to ensure a smooth transition for the little one. They named the baby Emily after her maternal grandmother, Emily Smith.

It didn't take long for tragedy to strike the tiny family. Johnie went to work as always, but his horse bucked him off while crossing a creek. Instead of returning home to change clothes, he performed a complete shift in sopping wet clothing. Johnie got home to find baby Emily Mae suffering from cold chills. He ignored his troubles, riding endless miles on horseback for the medicine his infant desperately needed.

The baby survived completely unscathed, but Johnie did not. The dunk he suffered into the creek set into his lungs. Pneumonia resulted, and a local doctor called in. Reaching the community took six days on horseback, but it was too late. Johnie died on Emily's first birthday, January 20, 1932.

Nearly destroyed by the incident, Jemima wailed and mourned daily for her one true love. At the funeral, Emily said "Da-da" while trying to get into the casket to be with her daddy. The period of adjustment seemed endless.

Jemima regaled her with tales of her gallant father and his short life as Emily grew. She recounted how the proposal went so well, but the wedding day did not. As Johnie prepped for the big day, the family mule got unruly.

Johnie gripped the reins tightly, but the mule won the battle. It rose and busted Johnie in the mouth, knocking him cold. Not a single tooth remained when he awoke in agonizing pain. The wedding party waited at the church, unaware of the drama.

Jemima, never known for patience, sent a search party of relatives out to find Johnie. As others reported Jemima's words, she'd gotten all prepped, and her man "was not gonna leave me lookin' right stupid at that altar."

The wedding was postponed for good reasons when the truth became known. Johnie healed up and kept his word.

On his deathbed, Johnie knew time was short. His request was that when Jemima got remarried, her beau could not lay one finger on his Emily. He made Jemima promise to discipline her only as long as she lived. Jemima kept that promise and relished it. She ruled with an iron fist.

A widow with an infant in rural Kentucky could only rely on family during tough times. The Brummett side ensured the fledglings were cared for. They let the two ladies move in as Jemima looked for work.

The 1930s saw a full slate of government programs spring up to give the people hope and employment. Jemima applied for the Works Progress Administration (WPA), unsure of the pay or working conditions. She'd refuse no work.

Jemima learned she'd travel to work in the program, planting trees, building parks, and learning skills across Kentucky. She loved taking walks with her little girl when time allowed.

On a stroll one day, Jemima grabbed a willow tree branch she used as an impromptu toothbrush. She dipped one end into the tin of snuff she carried religiously, then scrubbed her teeth as they walked along. Emily, in the age of curiosity, wanted the same. Spitting and chuckling as she went, Jemima agreed to let her little gal get a pleasant taste for posterity.

Emily could not wait to be like her mother and excitedly got a chunk of the ground snuff big enough to choke a horse. Jemima stepped back as Emily went to work.

Emily excitedly crammed the end of the stick in her mouth and scrubbed enthusiastically. She learned how to run the rod across even the back teeth from her mother. One stroke too far back caused the little lady to choke, spit, and vomit!

Jemima grabbed the stick from her child and doubled over in uproarious laughter! Little Emily stood by the roadside, vomiting as her mother sat down to enjoy the scene.

"See, big girl, you just can't do everything the big folks can do! You gotta do some growin' before you can be like full-growed people! That'll learn you!" Jemima muttered between belly laughs.

Jemima worked months on end, arriving home when she could. She carried apples, oranges, and chocolate bars in her personal satchel. Sometimes, Emily and her paternal grandparents visited the camps Jemima lived in.

Jemima got credit at a corner country general store for the grandparents to take Emily when she yearned for her favorite Pepsi, crackers, and bologna sandwich combination. That highlighted the long months of separation.

Having a dog to play with kept Emily occupied, too. She named him "Boss," and it suited him well. He provided protection and wrestled with his girl every day. Folks were alarmed at the apparent canine aggression.

"Hey, Jaybird, that child will get killed by that animal someday if someone don't stop this horseplay!" An alarmed neighbor pointed out.

"That child is not bein' killed, dummy! He's playin' as he always does. Why, that animal wouldn't hurt her for the world! He even kept an eye on her and pulled her back into the bedroom when I went workin' them fields! You worry about you, understand that? If you don't you may find yourself walkin' sideways, understand?" Jemima shot back firmly.

The man wisely moved away from the impending storm known as Jemima's temper. Being a single mother living in poverty added stresses that exacerbated her problems. She struggled mightily.

The weather challenged rural people with little in the way of possessions. The only way to accurately judge atmospheric conditions meant scanning the sky or checking old folk's arthritic bodies. Flash floods and tornadoes were a constant threat to life and limb. There appeared to be no escape from either.

The sky darkened one summer day, so much so that people lit oil lamps to see in their homes. Jemima took down her laundry in a hurry as the wind picked up. The day proved critical to their survival.

Inside the tiny cabin, the roof shook, and rain powered down. Lightning flashed, and the wind blew hard in a storm of biblical fury on the impoverished community. Jemima dared to look out to see a river of debris heading in her direction. She grabbed Emily and went outside, climbing to higher ground. Emily screamed as the storm hammered down. The footing could have been better as Jemima struggled up the steep grade. Big Bull Creek came to life as a science fiction monster to get the pair!

The flood menaced the area, mercilessly plucking anything in its path. Chicken coops, wagons, lumber, and logs sped by rapidly. Jemima's slip down a hill while carrying her child almost added to the watery catastrophe.

The adventurous child athletics Jemima used to ward off advancing suitors in her early days rose to the occasion. The fear and her abnormal physical strength allowed her to balance Emily on her shoulders so her child wouldn't get wet. Jemima stood straight up and deposited Emily onto a tree branch that held its ground against the rush of earth and water.

The doom surrounding the two dropped as they climbed higher in the tree and surveyed the area around them. The devastation left a swath of litter in a bubbling cauldron. The brush with immediate death made Jemima hold her little one tighter as the storm subsided.

The cabin did well against the Hell unleashed on it. Jemima and Emily made it back to find wind-strewn items everywhere.

They visited the general store the next day to commiserate with community members.

Folks were lost, never to be found again. Livestock disappeared from every farm. Hogs revered by everyone for their "rooter-to-tooter" versatility were gone in mass. When and if recovered, there'd be no specific brands to say who the owners were. Picking up the pieces and getting on with life became a full-time experience. One missing cousin of Jemima's (Name withheld) was found, and she celebrated in her "no-filter" style.

"Well, I heard today that my cousin got picked up yesterday by a twister on one mountain and ended up on another one! He got what little brains he showed scrambled so's nobody'd know the difference with him! That *tetched* (Crazy or touched in the head per Appalachian lingo) boy become nutty as a lake loon anyways! Lord, he's a lucky one, I reckon!" Jemima declared to the other shoppers.

A youthful, feisty single widow raising a child alone in rural Kentucky meant that Jemima needed a suitor, and one came calling in customary practice. Willie Smallwood, a handsome, tall, thin coal miner hardened by his occupation and the reality of the Great Depression, appeared. Being a distant cousin meant familiarity from the start. Could Willie tame the wild one?

Jemima's suspicions of the male species started from birth. Advanced thinking in the battle of the sexes meant that she took no guff from anyone, especially men. She told suitors that she'd be respected, or they'd be castrated, tarred, feathered, or plain *dead*! Men walked lightly in her presence if they had any sense at all.

Willie liked the fire he saw in her. He didn't want a handmaiden to keep as a prize to show others what he'd won. He wanted a Kentucky girl with grit and zero fear of the future if he got serious about anyone. Tough times created equally resilient people!

Jemima made courting complicated by having a child to dispatch to nearby relations. The accommodation was made to ensure that the two people spent time talking about the future. Jemima feared nothing but made her feelings known about being a miner's wife. Being a widow once was plenty for the independent lady. Willie promised to go in a different vocational direction somehow.

Without much fanfare, the proposal came quickly. Willie found a gem in Jemima Smith. Her terse, open-book style meshed with his quiet humor and unshakeable optimism. The man didn't know what he acquired, yet he went willingly.

On July 20, 1935, the pair married to both families' cheers. The couple seemed a good fit, and the proof was a volatile forty-four-year relationship. Years later, Willie became the referee between his bride and stepdaughter. His thick skin proved invaluable.

Jemima's days of scraping by with her temporary government job ended as a newlywed. She took to hoeing corn for one quarter daily on prosperous folk's farms. Willie went to his mine job, wondering if he'd return. Poorly lit with foul air, a collapse came with little warning. Strikes and violence were a way of life that gave no permanence. Rumors about Willie witnessing the war-like atmosphere firsthand were not confirmed because he'd never discussed it. As the strong, silent type, he remained tight-lipped his entire life.

Two stints in the mines and Willie investigated farming. His venture as a chicken farmer collapsed shortly into the business. As the family tired of eating "yard bird" for months, Willie's brother approached him with an exciting opportunity that paid well: moonshine running, or "moon-runnin" as named!

Willie drove anything he could get his hands on. The man pushed mechanical items to their limits, from farm tractors to cars and trucks. He demanded performance and would've been adept at racetracks across the South if only given a chance.

Willie's brother Buck was tired of the hardscrabble life Kentucky gave its residents. Tall and handsome, his love for fast cars and his mechanical abilities made him perfect for moon-runnin'. The job benefits were the fun of outrunning law enforcement officers and other drivers. Buck presented an easy sell to his little brother. A backslap, handshake and wide grins sealed the deal.

Willie knew that John Dillinger preferred Ford cars on America's developing system of roads. Modifications fell mostly on Buck, as Willie relished the role of test pilot. Concealing the precious cargo meant adding wider-than-stock tires to support the added weight and hidden compartments. Model A Ford parts were plentiful and took well to performance changes. The suspension simplicity and large trunk made the Ford near-perfect. Knowledge of the backroads kept the local boys employed and miles ahead of the law. Moon-runnin' cars were the first hot rods!

Although Prohibition was repealed in 1933, the most cash per week came from running the 'shine, as called by the populace. Willie and Jemima got quite good with their homebrew recipe and kept costs down. The price of government-sponsored alcohol remained stubbornly high, with taxes and "legalese" to endure. Repeal or not by the federal government, plenty of cash awaited the willing. Jemima didn't have much to say about the money coming in and never did, even in her later years. She'd only say, "Young'un, we did what we had to survive. You'd do the same thing! Nary, a word more will be said about it." Smart people dropped the subject.

Lazy Sundays were an optimal time to run liquor on the Christian Sabbath. Who expected deliveries, with many taking their day of rest and worship? Moonshiners counted on the authorities to back off and always wore their Sunday best as they distributed mountain dew.

Jemima sometimes traveled with her husband and brother-in-law duo in illegal activities. On this given Sunday, she tagged along but kept herself low in the backseat as the 'shine got unloaded. After a couple of rounds, she needed a bathroom.

"Willie, y'all gonna find me a place to piss and really soon! Them roads and these curves and bumps are killin' me!" Jemima shrieked.

"Jaybird, you gonna have to hold it in! Ain't no place out here for no rest room. Dang, why'd we bring her Willie?" Buck shot back.

Willie nodded and muttered about stopping when they could, but they were *working*. The miles went on, and Jemima wasn't silent.

"Boys, y'all gonna have a durn mess back here soon if you don't stop! After girls have kids, well, it ain't so easy to keep this stuff in!" Jemima yelled again.

Willie drove into a small village and parked behind a hardware store. He and Buck exited the car to empty the trunk. They told Jemima to stay put. They'd hurry back soon.

Poor Jemima suffered labor-like pains awaiting a rest stop. One glance at the floorboards of their hillbilly hotrod, and she saw a way out of discomfort. Yes, a quarter-sized rust hole meant instant bladder release! A river of life flowed out of her and onto the street. Free at last, Jemima rested comfortably while the boys dallied somewhere else.

Buck and Willie strolled up to the car but hesitated to get in immediately. Buck saw something disturbing under the vehicle.

"Willie, you look at that leak! Dang it, I thought we'd changed them radiator hoses last week! Quick, man, open that hood. It better not be the water pump!" Buck spoke softly.

Willie got the hood open to give the once-over to find the leak. Both men squeezed the warm hoses and found nothing. Buck got on his knees, put his fingers in the fluid, and then put it to his lips.

"Good God almighty, Willie, it ain't nothin' but *piss*!" Buck bellowed.

"What in the world? Oh, my Lord, Buck, you know how that got there, I reckon!" Willie answered.

Inside the car, one youthful lady rolled around, ecstatically holding her stomach. She concealed the snickers that became full-blown laughter as the men opened the doors!

"I told you, fellers, I had to...go!" Jemima said, shaking with spouting guffaws the men found increasingly annoying. Jemima never again went on any other runs after the episode. She didn't seem to mind, ever.

The risks with moon-runnin' were jail time, the danger of getting hurt behind the wheel, or death. Willie and Buck understood the chances they took daily. Still, the federal government, state, and local police departments were getting sophisticated. Technology evolved to the point of serious intrusion into the business, so the two brothers hung up their spurs for the final time. Going legit didn't necessarily mean giving up thrills. Those came in different forms.

As the whim hit them, the Smallwoods cat-and-mouse game of living in Ohio or Kentucky only created angst in everyone and went on for years. Willie finally grew weary of mining, farming, and the daily grind of scraping by in Kentucky. With two ill parents to care for, his options were few. One sibling went to Akron, Ohio, for a better life. When the invitation to join him came, Willie packed up the clan and moved again to Ohio for good.

World War Two
Chapter 4

The crisis of the Great Depression gave way to the reality that war in Europe might involve the United States in one form or another. The distaste for another European war meant many Americans preferred to stay on the sidelines. Industry, roaring back from the dead, needed people willing to add to the stockpile of democracy.

Defense plants in Akron, Canton, and Cleveland provided work for everyone. As the Allied Forces in Europe suffered tremendous blows from the German war machine, America's industrial might took notice. Every weaponry started in a plant somewhere, and Ohio's resources churned out hardware at a breakneck pace. Warm bodies dedicated themselves to long hours in steamy conditions year-round to ramp production and provide a comfortable living. My maternal grandparents were no exception. They took Akron and held it with both hands.

Emily went to school daily while Willie and Jemima rode to their defense jobs together. The monstrous building's humidity increased in the summer and produced indoor rain. No matter what the plant brought, it gave the duo more stability than moonshine running or coal mines and lent itself more profitability than farming.

The little family felt wealthy with a full refrigerator and stomachs to match. More kinfolk from Kentucky made the pilgrimage to a better life and arrived with open arms. Regular housing shortages began in Akron.

A few years of good life made my grandparents think long-term about the area they'd warmed to. Both knew Ohio as a land of milk and honey, but real estate costs far exceeded what the Bluegrass State charged for acreage. A duplex came on the market, so Willie put the down payment on it. Confident family could rent one side from him if no one else wanted to; Willie took the plunge as a homeowner and property owner. Good times arrived!

The new home away from the apartment dwelling proved a godsend. Having neighbors on only one side became a bonus infinitely better than over and under. For the time being, the family enjoyed settling in.

One night near midnight, Emily, now a curious child, came running from her bed to her parent's door, yanking it open with force. Something spooked her, and she shook as she dove into their bed.

Jemima, startled to feel the bed moving, asked what happened. Under the safety of handmade quilts, Emily stuttered while getting her breath.

"Mommy, I...I...I heard a boogeyman! I...swear! It has big, heavy boots and...went down the stairs!"

Willie came to his senses gradually, and he stumbled from bed, grabbed his pistol, and cleared the house of anyone living or dead. Nobody came into view.

After the reassurance, the bed kept the trio in slumber until morning. Jemima made breakfast, mindful that her little girl heard something nobody could talk her out of. Skeptically, she began an interrogation of her daughter.

"Emily, just what did you think you heard last night? Willie and I didn't hear a doggone thing!"

Emily described the sound of heavy boots going downstairs in the house. It sounded like a drunk wandered in and shuffled their feet to the basement. Everyone stayed on guard for weeks, but nothing happened until Jemima heard it herself one night. Emily streaked into the bedroom and didn't have to say a word. Willie slept like an infant.

Jemima sneaked from the bed, unafraid of man or beast and not searching for Willie's firearms. Seriously, nothing she'd met matched her.

The anger at being awakened made Jemima edgier as she wandered around the home. Almost wishing she'd have someone to eradicate, she stopped to assess her keen hearing. A step...then another...then...

Jemima stepped out of the shadows, grabbed the basement door violently, flicked on a light, and saw absolutely nothing. Emily cried in the commotion, and Willie came toting his loaded pistol.

"Jaybird, what in tarnation are you doin' creepin' into the basement this time of night?" Willie said with enthusiasm.

"Willie, I hate to agree with a little one, especially ours, but somethin' is goin' on in this place and it ain't from this world! We got an old haint livin' here with us! And you know durn well what I mean!" Jemima blurted out.

Both parents did what they could to calm Emily down. After much thought, prayer, and consultation, the situation recalled Jemima's upbringing.

She did not intend to live in a haunted house, especially with no rent from the mysterious squatter.

As Willie and Jemima reflected on their travels in life, neither missed coal mining camps nor the WPA accommodations. Ohio charmed in its own way despite variances with the Kentucky hills. Willie got used to the Buckeye State faster than Jemima but pledged to get the family land in a rural setting as soon as possible. Living off the land could not have been better for Jemima. Still, she kept the constant threat of another Depression in her mind. She needed to stay prepared.

"Willie Smallwood, we got us a nice place and all, but we gonna need to stretch out sooner than later! I mean, we gotta keep ourselves from starvin' here like we done down home. And make no mistake, whatever we get into, we gonna have the new place swept clean so's no boogie man lives with us ever again! I done had a bellyful of them, I have!" Jemima insisted.

"Jaybird, we're workin' our behinds off now, so I don't believe we got much time to look around or be picky! Old haints? Well, I'm not fond of them either! We sure don't need any of them follerin' us around!" Willie said.

"Just so you know, Willie, you better bring home ever cent of your checks so's we can save up! I'm doin' the same thing since I don't wanna be cramped with all these durned people around us, all wantin' to know our business!" Jemima yelled.

Months passed, but Jemima kept the pressure on. She and Willie worked day and night, saving as much as possible to escape city life. Their outspoken daughter demanded two requirements- indoor plumbing and electricity!

"Mommy, I think Ohio is growin' on me! Seems everyone has runnin' water, electricity, and flush toilets! Are we livin' high on the hog here or what?" Emily asked.

"Well, we ain't never gonna be rich, little one, but we doin' okay right now. We got a place in the country we're gonna see this weekend. As far as all them conveniences, well, you lived without 'em before, so you better not get too used to 'em, understand?" Jemima replied.

Willie drove his truck into the driveway of a country home days later. It needed work, but it didn't matter. The family got out, looked at the grounds, and rejoiced. The home displayed much better inside, complete with the modern living Emily desperately wanted. Jemima glanced through the rooms, silently praying as she went.

"Uh, Mister Realtor, has there been any funny things goin' on in this house? I mean, you know, uh...ghosts or deaths inside it?" Willie asked bluntly.

The realtor seemed surprised by the inquiry. The house was only about twenty years old and vacated by an elderly, church-going couple. No, he'd heard of nothing paranormal.

Jemima felt relieved as Emily picked out her bedroom, where to put her dog, and where she'd run in the fields out back. The place seemed too good to be true.

Willie signed the papers the same day to rent the property as soon as possible. The house meant a longer drive for Willie and Jemima, but neither cared if they could put crops in the ground. Their fierce independence grew from an upbringing of want and rationing.

Settled in, Jemima got Emily back into the school system, but hit-and-miss education didn't help. The family's nomadic existence left Emily behind kids her age in academics, so Jemima got her registered.

The simple act of getting Emily into the local public schools in Cuyahoga Falls proved the easy part. Emily's introduction by the teacher came with snickers from classmates. Her teacher didn't consider Kentucky education standards equal to Ohio's and said it in front of everyone. Emily burned with anger as she sat there.

Kids teased as they always do. When the bell rang and school was dismissed, Emily went outside for the short walk home. The trouble began with those first steps outside.

"Hey, hillbilly, why don't you go back to the hills where you belong?" One boy teased loudly.

Emily picked up her pace, striving to ignore him. More kids gathered, and the chants picked up in intensity.

"Hillbilly...go back home! Your mama's got your cornbread baking! Daddy's sloppin' the hogs 'til you get home! Hee-haw and thank you for visiting real schools!" one girl said.

Emily's temper wasn't as short as her mother's, but the teasing pushed her to murder! The war started when three boys knocked her down in the grass from behind!

"Y'all better hope when I get up that you can outrun me, since I'm gonna beat all your brains in!" Emily screamed.

The kids stood around and laughed at the threat as Emily gathered her books and lunch bucket, her only weapon.

The boys surrounded her and teased her mercilessly.

"Come on, hick! Do somethin' about us! You know you ain't got a chance!" Another boy shouted.

Emily corralled one of the boys with a tree, and he ran into it face-first. She swung the lunch bucket wildly into the boy's face, back, and chest. The girls ran away screaming as two boys tried prying her off the victim!

"Hey, now. We're just teasing! One guy said, let him go!"

Emily turned swiftly and, with righteous anger, went after anyone in sight.

"I'll give you what a hillbilly is for! You're nothin' but cowards! You wait 'til my mother gets hold of you; you wait!" Emily screamed.

The kids gathered the injured boy and ran back towards the school. Emily only cried when out of sight and got home shaken and dirty. A reckoning date came due!

When Emily cleaned up, Jemima was outraged! She and Willie changed clothes and went to school. Fury awaited the principal and staff.

Jemima nearly ran into the school, dragging Emily with her. Willie parked the truck and knew trouble had begun. No way could he stop his bride.

"What the Hell kinda school you runnin' here, people? My girl's beat up, shoved around, and mocked on the first doggone day? You better do somethin', and fast, because if I get my hands on them young'un's, I'll tear 'em all to pieces!" Jemima screamed in the school office.

The principal was taken aback but spoke up.

"Ma'am, uh, I am not sure what happened, but we'll get to the bottom of it. None of our students will get away with any mistreatment of others." The man insisted.

Jemima gave her famous death stare as Willie stepped around her and spoke.

"Fella, our child needs an education and we'll be durned if she's gotta fight for it each day! There's no call for anyone treatin' Emily like dirt!" Willie crowed.

"Sir, I assure you both that we do not condone these actions. But, that said, you know kids will be kids." The principal reminded.

Willie stood there with his mouth agape, but Jemima stepped around the principal's desk and closed in on the man's ear.

"Looky, here, Mister Big Shot principal, with all your schoolin' you ain't very smart! These kids treated my girl like she-it and they're gonna pay, if I must track 'em down like dogs! Words ain't gonna do a durn thing, are they?" Jemima threatened.

The principal stood up, sweat ran down his brow, and his face turned ghostly pale. He knew the Smallwoods were not ones to make empty promises to. He pledged to find the troubled kids and make them apologize.

"Well, I reckon that's nice, but like my wife says, these kids need a switch taken to them right away! Don't make us come back here mister, or you'll need to call the law to stop us from making things right ourselves! Got me? Huh?" Willie said.

The scared man agreed to the terms he'd heard. Willie and his family got into the truck. Jemima cussed the whole way home. Emily cried, saying the school wasn't for her just yet.

The fight for jobs and housing for those with a Southern accent kept things interesting. Subtle prejudices meant that families coming for employment in Ohio frequently went to the bottom of the priority list. Some native Buckeyes worried openly about displaced Kentuckians' takeover of the cities. Like any great upheaval of humanity, fears and distrust were common even in prosperous Akron. Clannish behavior from all concerned did not help.

"Jaybird, my brother called and told me my folks ain't gonna last much longer!" Willie said.

Jemima nodded in agreement, knowing that moving was the last thing anyone wanted. They'd managed to bank money with their good-paying jobs but starting again down south meant returning to their own biblical Egypt. The wilderness of scraping by, struggling, and caring for the elderly strained the little family. Jemima knew the reality facing them.

"Willie, our folks ain't gonna be around forever, that I can guarantee! We married richer or poorer, in sickness and in health, right? So, let's tell the property owner we got kin to care for and see what he says. But you gotta promise me you ain't gonna be minin' or runnin' 'shine when we get there,

Willie Smallwood! We need to farm to feed ourselves. I will take whatever work I get to help you. Your folks have been good to us!" Jemima said.

Willie faced the situation with dignity, as he always did. The property owner understood and let them out of their lease. The jobs at the plant went to others in need. Willie and Jemima thanked their bosses, said their goodbyes, and left without burning bridges.

No amount of love nor money kept the Smallwoods in Ohio. Kentucky called, they answered, and Emily hated moving again but understood that the only thing keeping Willie from military service was his elderly, infirm parents in the hills. The family came first, so back to the Bluegrass State they went.

Beautiful Ohio I
Chapter 5

Kentucky and Ohio grappled with the family for far too long. The moves to and from created heartache. Which state won out? The months after World War Two meant the Buckeye State kept the upper hand, with Akron the return engagement again.

Jemima and her daughter Emily were like fire and water, constantly on display for all to see. They could not agree on the time of day! Willie became the unfortunate pawn in the power struggle in which he usually refused to take sides. His quiet demeanor and peace-loving spirit were crushed by the competing tsunamis from his wife and stepdaughter. The quiet man needed body armor for daily living.

Jemima told others of her simple faith and devotion to her family. She lived by the motto "what goes around comes around" in life. Her biblical warning of "you reap what you sow" came to her from uncomplicated living in survival mode her entire life. Nothing she'd ever achieved was given to her; she earned her way in a rough-and-tumble male-centric world not ready for her views on womanhood or equal rights. Her universe displayed black and white, with no grey allowed.

Emily became more defiant in her pre-teen years, and once a teenager, she ached for more of the world. She knew her mother didn't see the world the same way she did, but she didn't care. The family lived a generational curse for the world to witness.

Willie knew Johnie's deathbed prohibition kept anyone from disciplining Emily but Jemima. Willie sided with his teen stepdaughter when he could. Jemima's death grip on "spare the rod, spoil the child" meant even minor offenses were dealt with harshly. Willie demanded discipline but did not believe in brutality. His so-called "interference" led to brawls with his spouse and others.

An Akron dance hall opened, and the entire clan checked it out one Saturday night. The simple place to unwind, have fun, and dance proved memorable. Emily danced with a cousin affectionately known as "Peanut," kicking her heels in style. Everyone approved except the club owner.

The owner should have been happy with a packed house on the weekend. Wary of the clientele, the Kentucky clan made him nervous when a dozen darkened the doorway. With any sense, the man should have stuck to having cash customers as a blessing. He chose otherwise and paid the price.

After seeing the teens dance away, the man approached and asked them to tone things down. If Jemima and Willie saw no sin in the dancing, why did he? The world may never know.

"Mom, that man says he don't like me and Peanut dancin' together in here," Emily said, pointing in the owner's direction. Jemima gave the stink-eye to him and spoke.

"Don't you worry none. If he gets outta line, I don't care if he owns Akron; he'll be one, sorry man!" Jemima promised.

Things cooled briefly as the family traded jokes, stories, and barbs about one another. Peanut and Emily hoofed it back onto the floor to show off and enjoy their night.

The owner pulled the kids aside and more forcefully made his commands known. He did something risky, and his night ended abruptly.

Willie and Jemima flew into action. Both circled the owner with angry rhetoric and defiance. The combination of Smiths, Smallwoods, and Freemans gathered in alliance spelled doom for the dance hall.

"Listen, bud, these young'un's are enjoyin' life, not hurtin' anyone with their dancin' one bit! I'm beggin you to back off before somethin' terrible happens!" Willie warned.

Jemima possessed zero diplomacy. She went for the man's jugular and made no bones about it!

"My husband's nicer than me, understand? If you don't want to get hurt, leave these kids alone!" Jemima promised.

The indignant man felt insulted and outraged by anyone standing up to him. He kept bouncers around, and while he did not want to use them, his honor was at stake.

"Look, I don't want trouble here, but I own the place, and nobody is gonna question what I say or do in here, especially you *hillbillies*! You can get out or my boys and I will make you!"

My grandparents didn't take to threats well. Both were tougher than shoe leather and seasoned to manage whatever life threw at them. Nobody recalls who put out the first blow, but a brawl of biblical proportions broke out instantly!

Emily and Peanut fled the dance floor and hugged the club walls for dear life as chairs were thrown, tables tipped, and mayhem played out! Glass broke, along with faces, noses, and egos, as the family clan gave a good account of their Appalachian roots. Blood covered the floors when the police arrived. Many dropped their activities, but not Jemima.

Jemima kept a grip on the hall owner's wife, who stood beside him, looking down on the family. Jemima vowed to teach a lesson the woman never forgot!

Police whistles blew, and bodies scattered, some getting up and out of the way faster than others. Nobody wanted to arrest the tired souls, but order needed to be restored.

Jemima held firmly to her opponent's hair, cussing the proverbial blue streak as she went.

"Doggone you, hold still so's I can get a better grip on this mop of yours! How you feelin' about hillbillies about now, you worthless piece of she-it?" Jemima shouted.

It took three cops to separate the only two people still fighting, both females. A police wagon, sirens wailing, showed up with an ambulance in tow. The police officers shuffled the men around, barking orders everyone understood immediately. Jemima's reckoning continued yet undone.

"Why I'll pull your durned head clean off, you scumbag! Wait 'til they take us away! She-it, I'll finish you off in that wagon! I'll make you walk like a kangaroo! Damn you!" Jemima screeched.

Her opponent, fearful even with police protection, tried to hide among them. She adjusted her ripped clothing and winced from the whippin' she'd received. Willie spoke up, trying to get Jemima to calm down.

"Jay, just be quiet and hush! We done what we *had* to do!" Willie emphasized.

Jemima took the warning with a grain of salt, lunging at the woman she wanted more than a piece of. One police officer's patience ran out, so he took his wooden club to Jemima's head. She descended like an elevator on the one-hundredth floor, and the police officers carried her to the wagon. Willie came unglued!

"Well, you scumbags! Why on top the earth did you hit my woman with that club? Y'all better call some more police in here!" Willie said with vigor.

The threat subsided as Willie got shoved into the wagon beside his "napping" wife and family members. The ambulance team bandaged the worst wounded as another police wagon showed up to take the club staff to the station. Peanut and Emily, wide-eyed and shocked, were questioned by police and released on the spot.

Jemima woke with a throbbing skull later. Willie prayed his little woman survived and that the charges were minor. As the clan sat in jail, nursing their traumas and contemplating the future, they realized their rivals were still at the local hospital. Anyone repentant? Hardly!

"Jaybird, you showed 'em what you can do, and it's why I always take precautions about rilin' you up too much! Man, that club will never forget you!" Willie mused.

The family's laughter continued inside the jail as the police gathered charges for the outbreak. It wasn't funny on Sunday morning. The family took their lumps in stride, paid their fines, and moved on. They were confident that the club owner didn't disparage Kentuckians ever again. The club crew experienced "southern discomfort," a bitter taste.

Emily's pursuit of modern life soldiered on, complete with makeup and earrings that put Jemima into a full breakdown stage. Her little girl matured, and an unspoken jealousy erupted between mother and daughter. Regardless of psychological interpretation, violence ensued when the duo disagreed. A running woodchipper was a safer place to be.

Emily's flirtations with boys made Jemima uncomfortable, and she determined to squelch the issue as often as needed. On a fall day, Willie raked leaves outside the rental home he'd found for the family. He couldn't have anticipated what came next.

As Willie took care of the fall cleanup of the property, Emily popped out the door with a cold drink for her stepdad. Dressed but with a physical maturity beyond her years, the next-door neighbor came out to greet them both.

"Gee, I've been meaning to get over and see you folks, but work's been crazy! I'm Boyd, and I'm glad to see the place rented!" The friendly neighbor announced.

"Well, I'm Willie Smallwood, Willie to most folks. I'm a carpenter for the Debartolo Company outta Youngstown. The work's good and I'm in the union. We just come back from Kentucky to stay; I believe." Willie responded.

"Yeah, I'm in the mechanic's union, and I love it. Glad to have you folks here. Your wife here has waved over my way when she's been out. They do say blondes have more fun, my friend. You're a lucky guy!" Boyd said.

"What? Wait now, my wife's a brunette! This here is my daughter, Emily! Lord have mercy, you couldn't have messed 'em up worse than that!" Willie said with emphasis.

Emily took it all in stride, quite pleased as the stranger put his head down in embarrassment and apologized.

"Oh boy, won't mother love to hear this! Hahaha! If you ain't careful Mister Boyd, you'll get us all killed! She tries keepin' me on a short leash!" Emily laughed.

Standing in the shadows of an open window, Jemima sneered when she overheard everything. She moved outside quickly to make things right.

"Hey, mister, I'm Jaybird Smallwood, Willie's one-and-only wife! My little woman Emily tends to talk outta turn, thinkin' she's all growed up and such! Willie and I's the only adults in this here house." Jemima reminded.

Emily didn't take the insult lightly. Proud to be seen by someone as a grown teenager, she let her mouth get in the way.

"Mister Boyd, I'll be on my own soon enough, you watch and see! My mother only sees me as a child! Happens all the time," Emily shouted.

Jemima grew up in an era of hit-first, ask-questions-second, and smashed Emily right in the teeth in front of God and everyone. Boyd's head snapped in shock as Emily went down to the turf. She didn't stay down long!

"I've taken a bellyful of your rules, your hate, and your meanness, Mom, and I ain't takin' it no more!" Emily barked as she returned the blow to Jemima's face. Willie quickly stepped between them as Boyd ran off to his own property.

"That's enough, you two! Somebody will call the cops and they'll take you both away. You want that?" Willie screamed as he struggled with both wild women.

Both ladies clung to the saying, "I'm Irish, English, and Cherokee! I ain't afraid of nothin'!" Poor Willie, the referee, stood silently, wondering who'd make it out of the decade first. He wasn't the fix-it man and lived a tortured existence with constant friction.

"You little witch, I'll tear you to pieces someday, and you wait and see!" Jemima yelled.

"And your gonna find me gone someday and away from your hillbilly ways, Mom! You know I will." Emily replied.

"I tell you, child, I'd see you six feet under rather than a goin' about your whorin' ways! You better walk the line 'til the law says you can get your ass outta here!" Jemima said.

Willie tried to cool things off by reminding them they were mother and daughter. Both turned on him in a way that a hungry shark eyes a shipwreck!

"Dad, I done told you guys I'll marry the first forner (Translation-foreigner) who asks me! I don't care what he looks like or even if he's got a job! I wanna go my way and I will someday!" Emily fired off.

"You may do it, little lady, but I reckon it won't be today, got me?" Willie roared right back.

Jemima shook her head, asked God how he'd sent one such as Emily to destroy her life, and returned inside. Scenes like this were familiar for years afterward. Oh, joy and rapture!

Emily's constant up-tempo drive for a better life felt like Chinese water torture to Jemima. Nothing she did seemed good enough for her only child. At the root of it all, one house appeared not big enough for both. Emily needed to expand her wings somehow without dying in the process. Family members from the Bluegrass State held no sway in Emily's freedom quest, but they tried.

The most heinous battles ended when Jemima finally agreed to let Emily take a job. Willie knew he'd be unable to side much with either person or face double elimination from both women.

Jemima quietly contemplated the peace Emily's independence brought, but how could it suit everyone? Enter one *foreigner* from Pennsylvania who tossed out his lifeline. Emily caught it and ran!

When Emily met Gusty, the two teens fell as deeply in love as expected from a few meetings. They decided on a wedding and didn't care what anyone else thought.

Jemima called it all foolishness and "puppy love," but it mattered little. Willie wasn't sure about matrimony for anyone after his experiences. He even cracked jokes with Gusty when he got the chance.

"A man is standin' in church one day when the devil shows up beside him, tryin' to scare him good! The devil looks him over and says 'you ain't scared of me, huh?' The man cocks his head sideways and says 'nope, been married to your sister for thirty-two years now!' Hahaha! Ain't that a good one?" Willie asks.

"Haha, yeah, I love a good Satan joke! But the funny thing about jokes is that there's usually truth in 'em someplace!" Gusty said with questions in his mind.

"All I'm sayin' is that I wish you kids' good luck, and you especially! And a Baptist marryin' a Catholic, well, I heard tell that's a recipe for disaster no matter how you slice it!" Willie said confidently.

Gusty took the advice and held it tight as another male headed into something he knew nothing about. He figured he'd learn along the way. He expected the same from Emily.

Not long after the two youngsters married, Gusty got tired of finding Emily at her mother's house. It didn't make sense to him that the one person who longed for her freedom returned to the nest. The situation worked itself out when the lovebirds got another apartment out of sight from Jemima's watchful eyes.

Parenthood came upon the newlywed couple in a hurry. Both families were excited to have offspring coming, but one person kept her doubts- Jemima!

"Willie, I am nervous about them havin' a baby! They ain't been married a year yet! And I swear to the Lord above, I wouldn't trust Emily with a goldfish! Her mind wanders and how's she gonna raise a child? You got to be kiddin' me! Gusty's people shore ain't gonna know the real her like we do, you reckon?" Jemima asked.

"Now, now, Jaybird. Babies don't come with no instructions! All of us are gonna keep an eye on them. They'll be fine, I know it." Willie assured.

The usual celebration ensued when my sister Shirley arrived after nine months of matrimony. Everyone rejoiced at the blessed event. Emily and Jemima drew closer with the birth of the new baby girl. Shirley gave everyone a needed balm in Gilead for the family. (A Mamaw/Jemima and a Papaw/Willie came into existence years later.)

Jemima kept her granddaughter as often as possible, even being amazed by Emily's initial motherhood foray. Two short years passed, and my sister Linda came along. Trips to the promised land of Kentucky allowed Jemima to show off her girls like she never did for Emily. The root of bitterness took hold and could never be permanently killed.

As my sisters grew, they latched onto both sets of grandparents. While not an official popularity contest, the families took turns spoiling the girls as they could. Unfortunately, Shirley and Linda, the intended family balm, became the symbols of jealousy.

Jemima became the kids' protector, defender, and all-around savior when they faced the music for any of Emily's discipline. The contradictions and hypocrisy were not lost on Emily by any stretch.

"Mother, am I gonna be able to keep these girls in line or not? You did your beatin' to my brains I was a kid, but now these girls can do no wrong in your eyes! Lord help me, I just can't understand it!" Emily complained to Jemima.

Jemima nodded and smiled. She reached deep into her sarcasm bag and let the words fly.

"Hey, oh, Emily, you deserved every durn beatin' you got! Sassin' me? No way do I take that from anybody! You always gotta get that last word in, don't you? You been arguing since you could talk! I bet Jesus just shakes his head when you go on and on!" Jemima insisted.

Emily could not be the mother she anticipated, which got under her skin. The only resolution to the perpetuated jealousy might be solved in the grave one day.

Willie and Jemima doted on their granddaughters. The girls were faultless, a common theme grandparents grab ahold of. Frequent visits to candy shops and ice cream stores made permanent memories neither sibling forgot.

Jemima mellowed with her girls around. Her hearty laughter kicked into high gear with what her grandchildren said or asked. Willie was delighted as a grandfather and showed it in his soft-spoken manner.

The grandgirls spent the night as often as possible with Willie and Jemima. Breakfast meals meant crunched-up cornflakes, eggs, biscuits, gravy, and bacon each time. Jemima rose early and presented the meal at dawn, regardless of the season. And the two girls couldn't get enough of the hospitality.

An overnight stay on a Saturday meant church services were mandatory the morning after. The girls were far more comfortable with the Catholic presentation than the marathon Baptist services Willie and Jemima enjoyed. Linda couldn't be still for so long.

Jemima kept a pack of gum, Lifesavers, or candies to keep the girls busy, at least for a while. Linda's questions rose to the surface.

"Mamaw, why do these services go on and on? These things take forever!" Linda complained.

"Honey, some folks is slow to get the spirit, I reckon! Preacher man gets paid to say a lotta words and he ain't reached his limit! Hush, now!"

Jemima's world improved with her grandparents' duties. With Emily married off and doing well, Willie stood front and center in Jemima's world. One could even say he stood in the crosshairs of her aim, ready or not.

The Willie Wars
Chapter 6

Willie got into carpentry after the prosperity of WW2 wore off. Even with the Korean conflict, he set sights on a union job with a future. Willie found one in the DeBartolo Corporation out of Youngstown, Ohio. He felt like the king of the world with excellent pay and benefits as a naturally gifted builder. With Jemima in charge, he couldn't even be a prince.

Willie worked out of his Akron home in sites ranging from Columbus, Youngstown, and Cleveland to Ashtabula. The man worked before daylight each day and occasionally worked Saturdays, as necessary. His bride waiting at home for his weary soul provided comfort, but not always.

Willie took his usual bottle of ice-cold beer from the ice box on a hot Friday afternoon. His calling as a good-natured but reserved man still meant that he occasionally stirred the pot with his bride. Sometimes, he went too far.

A few more beers later, Willie got loose. His baritone voice, perfect in church, belted out the tune. It didn't reflect well as Jemima prepped their dinner.

"If you've got the money, honey, I've got the time, we'll go honky-tonkin', have ourselves a time! Bring along your Cadillac, leave my old wreck behind, cuz' if you've got the money honey, I've got the time! Yippee, yahoo, Oh ain't that a good one Jaybird?" Willie said, gaining volume as the song went.

Jemima stared at her man in a way reserved for someone facing death by misadventure. Her gaze and disgust only egged Willie into an attempted second verse.

"I say if you've got the money, honey, I've got the time, we'll go honky-tonkin', have ourselves a time." Willie's voice trailed off as the man got the hint.

"Now, Willie, you laugh, act a fool anytime you want, but I'll not be mocked, understand? You might have been singin' that stuff when you was out whorin' around as a youngster, but not now! I will not listen to the foolishness!" Jemima deftly replied.

Willie chuckled and continued singing, ever so low and under his breath. Jemima's perfect hearing would not be undermined by a man who'd dabbled in too much beer after being in the hot sun all day.

"Willie, you've gone enough now! If you wanna keep that head of yours where it lays, then shut up and shut it up now! She-it, I'd kill you dead rather than listen to that damn song!" Jemima ordered.

Full of spunk and Stroh's beer, Willie did not want his manhood questioned. He'd not stay silent.

"Jaybird, uh, Jemima, you know the Bible says the woman is to *obey* the man in marriage. Well, it's high time you learnt that! I bust myself daily to provide and come home to some fun occasionally. If you got the money, honey, I've got the time; we'll go honky-tonkin' and have ourselves a time!" Willie rambled as he tipped his head skyward in triumph.

When Willie *woke* the following day, he thought he'd really tied one on the night before. His head throbbed, and a goose egg protruded from his forehead. He staggered out of bed, unaware that he did not have to work. Then he went straight for aspirin to soothe his aching cranium while searching for his lunch bucket and thermos.

Jemima sat at the same table where the altercation started the evening before. She sipped coffee and waited for the storm to begin again.

"Whew, Stroh's beer never, ever hit me like that did last night, Jaybird! Man alive, it kicked jest like the 'shine we used to make! I drank my beers, then lights out! Wow!" Willie crowed, then remembered his severe headache.

"Willie, don't you ever start singin' that damn song about havin' money to go honky-tonkin'! and you know how I feel about bein' called my legal name! She-it, you skatin' on thin ice, old man!" Jemima retorted.

Willie looked around as she talked, unable to comprehend the non-work Saturday. His head felt like a car drove over it. And how did he get the bump on his noggin?

Jemima slyly told one of the biggest whoppers in marital relations, totally disregarding her handy, dandy cast iron skillet weapon. He got her "truth," which suited the situation.

"Willie, when you come home yesterday, you'd been in that hot sun all day! Then you started swillin' those beers, celebratin' Friday! Next thing I know, you're singin' and carryin' on. You got up from the table, fell over and smashed your durned head right on it! So, you ain't gotta work today, dumbass!" Jemima replied. Her secrets were tighter than an elephant wearing leggings.

The typical volatility of the relationship came out. The violence happened many times before. Their love provided *fracturing*.

The supernatural reared its head again in the Akron house Willie and Jemima lived in. Were the happenings related to attraction to these two, or were they simply unlucky in their home choices? The debate went on for over four decades.

Early morning, Willie awoke to the beautiful scent of fresh coffee from the kitchen. Rubbing his weary eyes, he saw Jemima stone cold asleep. "Huh, he thought; Bunt must've gotten up early and returned to sleep. Unusual for her!"

Willie dressed and moved so he didn't wake his bride. Upon arrival in the kitchen, the coffee pot sat unattended. No sign of movement anywhere. Could his "smeller" have just been off this day? No, the coffee woke him up. A rational man, he believed his mind played tricks on him.

Jemima got up with nothing to say about his revelation except that the homebrew from a family hopper in Kentucky still occupied the cupboard. At least *some* were still there.

"Willie, you been tappin' that stuff this early in the mornin, have you? My Lord, don't you start makin' up ghost stories! You know they don't scare me none! She-it Willie, she-it!" Jemima said with force.

"I'm tellin' you, Jaybird, that I smelt it this mornin' and no, I ain't tapped into no 'shine! I knew you'd been in there makin' the coffee!" Willie insisted.

"Well, I will tell you just once more that it weren't me, durn you! I don't appreciate you bringin' this ol' haint stuff up here. I sure as Hell don't want a boogeyman givin' us grief in this place. Now you know that place with them boots up and down the stairs was for shore haunted! After we moved out somebody found bones buried in the basement! That made all the Akron papers. No, no ghosts need to foller us here, I tell you!" Jemima said.

Both agreed to disagree on the paranormal in their home. Jemima said spirits naturally hung onto places. Willie wanted no part of it.

Shirley and Linda spent the night weeks later. The joys of grandparenthood were evident in the fun the foursome enjoyed. Hide and seek, eye-spy and board games left great memories. Bedtime came, and everyone drifted off to slumberland.

Linda rose first the following day, the smell of fresh coffee letting her know her grandparents were awake. She went to the kitchen expecting to see them, but they weren't there. Linda peeked carefully into the bedroom to see Willie and Jemima sound asleep. She waited in her room until both stirred, and she could tell them what had happened.

"Mamaw, it sure smelled like fresh coffee brewing in the kitchen when I woke up, but when I came in, nobody was here!"

Jemima shot her famous sideways glance at Willie as he opened his newspaper.

"Oh, uh-huh, I see. Willie, you been puttin' her up to say these things? I like jokes like everyone else, but this ain't funny, old man! You get her to lie to me and you know, I'll split your durn head wide open! I been fightin' since I come on this earth, and I'll go out the same way! She-it, you know it's true! "Jemima said.

Willie dropped his paper and peered into his wife's face, her eyes afire with the blackness of coming wrath. The man thought carefully about his answer. His life depended on it.

"Jay, you got it all wrong! I never said no such thing to her! There's somethin' goin' on in this place. I ain't lyin' -honest to God! There's a haint that's livin' in these here walls somewhere!" Willie answered.

Jemima knew all about ghosts, specters, and "haints," as Kentucky locals called them. She'd heard a ghostly organ playing at a deserted mansion way back in the hills as a teen. Her family farmhouse poltergeist vanished when they moved away...or did it? Things got weirder as time went on.

The granddaughters wanted to leave quickly from the place visited by things unseen. Ever the believer in all things paranormal, Emily didn't want her parents to miss out on the visits but put her girls first.

Weeks passed with nothing unusual until Jemima awoke to the smell of... freshly baked biscuits. The scent wafted into the room as Willie slept soundly. Thinking she'd imagined it all, Jemima lay there wondering. How could this be?

Not much in this world or any other will stop a hillbilly from a fresh-baked biscuit. Aliens could have landed and baked it. Jemima, the adventurer, wanted to discover the source of the issue.

A ghost making coffee or biscuits didn't sound threatening to anyone. It wasn't like other specters climbing stairs, opening doors, or rattling chains to scare the crap out of someone!

Jemima crept into the kitchen slowly, with not a creature stirring. She flipped on a light to ensure that nothing got past her. Jemima sniffed the aromatic scent without an earthly reason. She told Willie what she witnessed when he awoke.

"See, woman, I don't joke about them kinda things! Don't you ever tell me again what I smelled, understand?" Willie said sharply.

Jemima squinted her eyes and tipped her head downward, an intimidation tactic she had learned somewhere along the line.

"See here Willie Smallwood! I don't cotton to bein' talked to that way and of all people you should know it! I'll knock the fire out of you if you ever do it again! I'll do whatever I take a notion to and you or nobody else is gonna stop me! Only the good Lord can keep me quiet!" Jemima cried.

By this time, poor Willie walked away, grumbling under his breath something about why women were created in the first place, especially his. He tilted his head sideways and said aloud, "Why me, Lord," barely audible enough for the love of his life to hear.

"Willie, let's jest stop right here. If my grandkids weren't here, I'd take a run-and-go at you! No more triflin' today. Why, those poor girls get enough of that ol' foolishness at home!" Jemima added.

While the occurrences continued with the ghostly scents in the home, word came to Jemima that a woman "in trouble" needed a home for a child. Being a mother again at age fifty struck fear and loathing into many women, but not Jemima. Even with close relationships with her granddaughters, she longed for young'un's she could call her own. Undeterred and with no regard for Willie's feelings, she moved forward to adopt a little girl they named Frances. Another volatile mother-daughter duo kicked off in 1960, just in time for the new decade.

Willie knew he'd never change his wife's mind about taking on a child. At eight years Jemima's junior, the carpenter with the affable ways, great smile, and huge heart knew his wife well. Everyone adapted, and things rolled on, as they always did, in his "glass-half-full" view of life. Willie's love for people knew no earthly bounds.

The child proved quite a handful for her adoptive parents. Apprehensive at first, even Emily thought more children for her mother might be good overall and considered her new baby sister a blessing. Every child deserves to have a family to care for them.

Frances became a strong-willed toddler who frequently disobeyed both parents. Jemima followed what she'd been taught by disciplining Frances harshly as she'd done with Emily. Still, the consoler, Willie, only intervened when Jemima exceeded a pain threshold he hated. Attention deferred from himself, but the anger and dysfunction bruised another generation, literally and figuratively.

An incident years later at a playground highlighted the combat between Fran and Jemima in the child's upbringing. Not moving fast enough, Jemima's commands insulted her, and it always got an immediate reaction. Never pretty.

Fran's enjoyment and cackling at the swing Willie pushed her on were priceless. When it stopped, he told her to come along and eat lunch. Emily and Gusty were there with their kids at a picnic table and watched the scene unfold.

Jemima asked Willie if he told Fran to get off the swing. Of course, he insisted. He looked over, and Fran, an already obstinate four-year-old, displayed no intention of coming to eat. Jemima went for her favorite tree, cut a limb, and stripped it, making her weapon of choice come to life.

The whacks of the "switch" were heard across the park as families surveyed the grounds. Fran screamed a blood-curdling yell each time her mother brought the whip onto her flesh. A few swats sufficed, but not to Jemima as she mercilessly continued the pounding. Fran needed a lesson, with bloodshed and marks for memories.

Willie shook his head and yelled for Jemima to stop as Gusty left his table to step in. Adults pointed, rounded up their own children, and looked on helplessly. The scene turned the beautiful day very ugly. Gusty grabbed the switch from Jemima's grasp as several men approved his action. Jemima's red-hot anger only got worse.

"What the Hell are you doin' Gusty, huh? I will make my kids mind my way, thank you very much! Don't you ever put your hands on me again unless you want kilt, you hear me! Jemima screamed, Willie get your useless ass over here so we can take your daughter and go!"

The entire park went eerily silent as Willie tried apologizing to his son-in-law and daughter. Emily couldn't keep quiet.

"Mother, you don't make no sense! Always gotta hurt someone until they're near dead, don't you? Jesus, Mary, and Joseph, the eyes of the whole place are on us! Don't you ever threaten my man again, or you'll be the sorriest woman in Akron! You're lucky nobody called the cops! Damn, crazy woman!" Emily said as she glared in her mother's direction. Jemima seethed, promised war, and walked on.

The day's fun melted away. The families went their separate ways, talking about each other on the drive. Jemima threatened Willie with worse when they got home. It's nice to think of this as an isolated incident, but that is untrue. Brutality came in abundance in Jemima's DNA.

A few years passed, and again, Jemima heard another child needed a home. Up to his elbows in hot-headed estrogen, Willie wanted a testosterone balance. A boy came down the pike, and Willie rejoiced. Jemima called things even and agreed to the compromise. Deeper into her fifties, another reckoning came along in a boy named Timothy.

Tim fit in right away, chaos and all! (I hit the calendar directly between Fran and Tim.) He showed an accelerated growth pattern and a fun personality to match. The family rounded out and lived the American dream.

Independents Days
Chapter 7

With Akron behind my grandparents, my recollection of the Cuyahoga Falls, Ohio, days is memorable with Mamaw (Jemima) and Papaw (Willie). When I came along in 1963, the mini farm between Cleveland and Akron they cared for provided immense pride. Pens full of goats, rabbits, and guinea pigs aligned alongside the house. Chickens roamed like the nomads they are. Several acres of vegetables and fruits kept canning a top priority. Inside the old farmhouse basement housed breeding grounds for Boston Terriers. The settings provided loads of fun.

My Dad always carried his Colt automatic pistol to my grandparents' home because it provided room for target practice. Papaw took out his revolver and blasted a coffee can or water bucket he hung in the trees. Hands-over ears were as good as they got for hearing protection in the fields. Free-living in the "safety last" era is displayed for all.

Poor Papaw never caught a break from Mamaw's suspicious mind and jealousy. The man always noticed a mini-skirt or pretty lady gracing his places of travel. He didn't leer or make rude comments, but the all-seeing eyes of Mamaw prowled for an infraction. Mamaw kept a machete under her mattress on her bed just in case Papaw stepped out on her or wanted "tom-cattin," as she called it.

Mamaw's duty after getting Papaw out of the way meant getting my Aunt Frances to the bus stop. A neighbor lady across the street drew Mamaw's ire months before with the long stare she sent Papaw's way one sunny afternoon after he returned from work. The woman unknowingly made the list Mamaw inventoried daily. Ready or not, a battle bubbled under the surface.

Relative calm stayed until one autumn morning when Mamaw and her perceived single rival showed up at the bus stop simultaneously with their daughters. The lady nodded to Mamaw in a neighborly gesture most wouldn't take offense to. Mamaw did not fall into the category. Her accusing stare at the woman's outfit shined through.

"Woman, I saw you lookin' at my husband Willie, and I appreciated it none! Keep them eyes in your head when my man is around if you wanna keep 'em!" Mamaw barked.

The startled woman replied more calmly than she'd received.

"Ma'am, I have no idea what you're talking about. I don't even know your husband." The lady replied.

"Woman, I know a whore when I see one! I *know* you ain't got no man over there and mine's well-taken, understand? You mess up and I will put a hitch in yer git-a-long! With that outfit you got on if you crack a fart you'll fer sure split yer britches." Mamaw said forcefully.

"Look, we have children here and you shouldn't use that kind of language. What you think of me doesn't matter. Consider these kids." The shocked woman said.

"You been served notice, little lady! That's all I know. You make a move, and you'll regret it for the rest of your days! Why I'll knock you into next week, I will. If you don't watch out, I'll beat you like a Cherokee drum!" Mamaw thundered.

The woman's innocence or guilt is debatable, but what happened next made the local newspapers for months. The two women faced off, and tempers flared into a full-blown war after the kids made it onto the school bus and were out of sight.

Per my truthful grandma, the rival woman landed the first blow into Mamaw's face. Mamaw shrieked, tearing into her rival's clothing while punching like an octopus. A seasoned brawler, Mamaw cleaned house until...

...the younger gal reached into her purse for a weapon to end the beating! She found a flat screwdriver and drew it back in terror.

"You witch, you better make damned sure you kill me with that! If you don't you gonna meet your Maker!" Mamaw spoke defiantly.

The screwdriver plunged and gouged Mamaw's hands and arms as she fought valiantly to stay upright. The blood flew in crimson spurts with each stab she took. The carnage yielded more than twenty-five wounds when the attack ended. Mamaw lay in a pool of blood while her opponent retired inside her home.

How a woman in her early sixties regained her composure to crawl home is anyone's speculation. Wrapping her torn clothes around the wounds, she got an ambulance on the way. Scared neighbors heard her cries and called the sheriff's department. All Hell broke loose at the Smallwood home.

Mamaw's ambulance ride, punctuated with profanity, moved her in and out of consciousness. One moment, she'd scream for vengeance, then settle down and go back out. Occasionally, a prayer on her lips for her mortality sneaked through.

Local doctors marveled at Mamaw's resilience. Bleeding heavily, many folks passed out at this stage of pain and horror. Mamaw's tough, Kentucky mountain stock came to play twenty-four hours on any given day. Per Dad, Mamaw's meanness provided her with a superpower. A week in the hospital aggravated the staff, and my saintly grandmother exited. A score needed to be settled, and only the Good Lord could stop the coming slaughter.

A criminal case came about and was necessary for justice. Unfortunately for Mamaw, the perpetrator's attorney proved the fight a self-defense issue. Our family howled with rage about the apparent injustice. Rather than calling the clan together (Think of the film "Next of Kin") for a moment of comeuppance, Mamaw sought legal and civil means to hurt her antagonist.

The civil court case came to being once Mamaw fully recovered. The news made the Akron Beacon Journal with sensational headlines of the sordid affair. The accused woman's attorney mounted her defense by playing the client as a victim. They alleged that Mamaw landed the first blow, which played into the defense posture when the court came into session.

Papaw worked his job and could not be present. Shuffling forward, Mamaw put on a new dress and came out swinging. The Summit County Courthouse prepared for the Kentucky wildcat roaring out of her lair.

Mom and Dad took Mamaw to the courthouse for support, retribution, and payback. They wanted justice to be served and the press to report the facts. A sideshow, complete with clowns, devolved into chaos. No decency applied.

Opening statements read by attorneys on both sides spun the proceedings into high gear. Mamaw glared a hole through the adversary opposite her. Her counsel warned her not to get too animated in her hatred. It was a nice try by the well-educated but naïve professional man.

Mamaw could not hold her tongue in any fashion in her life. Things came from down deep, spewing like an exploding bomb. She fidgeted in her seat, and Mom leaned over to tell Dad the obvious.

"Gus, she's not gonna sit still this whole time! Mom cannot hold anything in. I am afraid of what she's gonna do! Why, they ain't got enough deputies in here! She gotta speak her piece! I know my mother!" Mom whispered in her loud style.

Poor Dad looked at her like she'd sniffed an entire glue bottle.

"Holy Christopher, Emily, I know all about the way she can talk. It runs in the damn family! It's all I know for sure. You might as well piss in the wind!" Dad replied confidently.

A brief recess came, and Mamaw moved toward her enemy. Still, watchful deputies stepped in between, reminding her she sat in a courthouse.

The court reconvened, and everyone took a seat. Mamaw went forward to the stand. With malice in her heart and eyes, she took the oath. Some say she left a permanent burn on the Bible where she placed her hand. (Not independently verified.)

The county prosecutor introduced himself and began a line of questions that irritated an already mad mountain woman. He asked if she knew the lady sitting in the courtroom.

"You mean that ol' whore in the blue dress over yonder? Yessir, I shore as Hell know that durned bitch! She-it, y'all are lucky I can't get my damn hands on her!" Mamaw bellowed.

The judge's shock set him back as the entire courtroom erupted in awe and hilarity.

"Misses Smallwood, I will not have that language in my courtroom, is that understood?" The judge warned sternly.

"Well, sir, I stand by what I said! She ain't no good and we ain't doin' nothin' but wastin' time and good money on her ass! She shore got lucky with that damn screwdriver, that's the dyin' truth!" Mamaw asserted.

The judge pounded the gavel with authority to regain order.

"Madam, please, refrain from profanity in this courtroom. I will have you removed if you persist, is that understood?" The judge asked.

"Okay, well, you wanted the *whole* truth and nothing but the truth, right? She-it, that's all I'm givin' here! I am healed up and we can settle this outside! She'd not last a New York minute, fer damn sure!" Mamaw replied.

More hoots and hollering came from the packed room. Mom shook off the embarrassment and ran into the lobby. She couldn't take any more of the honesty coming from her dear mother. The judge issued his last warning as he reclaimed the order that was perilously on the verge of collapse.

"I see that this is a contentious roomful of people. Folks looking to be entertained have been so, but I am not! If needed, I will clear this place of only the necessary ones to get this over. Is everyone clear? Misses Smallwood, I will hold you in contempt if you swear or stir this crowd any further. Do you understand?"

Mamaw nodded, but Dad knew she'd not be able to comply. He left to check on his shamed bride.

"Em-uh-lee, Jesus, Mary and Joseph, you know how your mother is! If she keeps this up, she'll be the one in handcuffs and a gag. Who could blame the judge? She sounds like a maniac in there! If that judge only knew." Dad said.

"Gus, she's a disgrace with what she's doin' in there. The other side ain't got much to prove to win this one. I just wish she'd play along and let that expensive lawyer earn his durn money! Her filthy mouth is gonna get her thrown right outta here!"

Dad nodded in agreement and added one last thought.

"Emily, people in Hell want ice water, don't they? I mean, Jesus Christopher, your mother don't know when to shut up! All she's gotta do is show those scars to the jury and its case closed. And I hate to go back in, but..." Dad said as Mom interrupted.

"We gotta go back in there, but I wish I'd brought me an ol' Halloween mask to wear! I sure as Hell don't want my face in the papers! What will the neighbors say? How are we gonna look to everybody? She's makin' a mockery of the court!" Mom interjected.

Image meant everything to my parents, but they could not leave Mamaw alone. They bucked their shame and went back into the lion's den.

The courtroom comedy-drama kept the jury interested. Even others in the crowd loved the entertainment value because Mamaw's raw language wouldn't make it to all the media of the day. A brief recess came for each team to reload.

Mamaw strutted into the lobby and found her two closest supporters. She could not keep silent or still. At least nobody threatened her outside the courtroom doors.

"You see how they're a moly-coddlin' that whore? Jesus, Lord, I aim to make her squirm in that seat every durn minute she's here! I'll be in her nightmares forever more, never lettin' her get a minute's peace! I told that lawyer we could save all this time by lettin' me have exactly five minutes with her in one of them cells! She'd see the light- I tell you!" Mamaw cried.

Mom and Dad only wanted her to see a good chance of winning if she let the law take its course.

"Jaybird, you just gotta keep that trap of yours shut while the jury takes things in! From what I see, they look to be on your side. I don't know if you can do it!" Dad mentioned.

Mamaw, undeterred, still wanted justice in her way. The woman with the weapon was as guilty as sin in her mind, but the jury awaited. Everyone filed back in to press on.

Mom leaned over to Dad with her usual insight and lack of discretion.

"Gus, I'm afraid if they let this woman off, my mother will destroy this entire courthouse! She's meaner than a bear missin' its cubs! You know it's true!" Mom spoke.

"Emily, holy mackerel, I know she can be a devil, but if she acts up, she's gonna be in jail. Safer for everybody. No matter what happens, that woman better move outta that neighborhood! Your mother will cut her up for fish bait and put her in Lake Erie!" Dad answered.

As Mamaw glared at her enemy, the proceedings began again. The judge kept a close eye on my granny, fully expecting her to sprint and pounce before anyone could stop her. Soon, the jury debated a decision, and no matter the outcome, someone went home unhappy.

The jury dismissed, and the world awaited their answer. Mamaw stared, mumbling a curse at her rival. The jury swiftly decided the case. Good news or bad for the family?

The presiding juror took his seat with others as they returned. The judge made everyone stand to read the verdict. The decisive moment arrived.

"We, the jury, rule in favor of the plaintiff, Jemima Smallwood, in this claim for damages, both physical and mental, in our judgment."

Mamaw let out a rebel yell, shouting to God and country, while the defendant collapsed in shock. The courtroom got as loud as a stadium crowd while the judge clamored for order. An undisclosed settlement came to Mamaw, but she was always tight-fisted about money.

Not long after, Mamaw's real or imaginary rival moved away for good. Our trips to Cuyahoga Falls were frequent and usually fun. Still, as I got older, my Mamaw insisted I appeared flawed, or to put it into plain, Kentucky slang-*Tetched*! (Not an endearing hillbilly remark!)

Everyone saw my father as my hero. He combed my hair like his. He bought suits for me that I proudly wore like him. Someday, I told everyone I'd smoke the same Winston cigarettes, drink the same coffee, and wear the same cologne as my idol. Big Gus and Little Gus were on display to everyone around us.

With Dad's example, I used his wisecracks and sarcasm in my formative years. It worked great with kids but didn't fly with adults, particularly teachers and grandparents. While Papaw's good-natured view of the world overlooked my offenses, Mamaw did not. Her comments went this way:

"Emily, that boy is *tetched*! He needs brain help and right away! You know I can't stand doctors, but that boy is somethin' else the way he carries on and acts-a-fool! I mean it, he should have someone lookin' at his dadblamed head! He plays the e-dit (Mamaw's earnest attempt to say idiot) all the durn time! He tries bein' his daddy, but it don't fly well with grown-ups! She-it, he's got problems!"

In our Stefanow family, I was an odds-on favorite to finish slightly above Phil in a popularity contest to win Mamaw's greatest affection. I eventually finished first, but it took decades to get there.

In the late 1960s, we partied with my grandparents. There were big Sunday dinners after church and horseshoe pitching in the shade. We took drives into the country to pass the time away, simply enjoying the company and scenery.

As I grew up, others grew older. The Kentucky family expected routine visits from the Buckeye deserters. The trips became more frequent when Mamaw's mother, Ma Smith, became bedridden in her nineties. Dad and Papaw took vacation time, and we set sail in a station wagon for the ever-long drive. Like a band of gypsies, we trooped south.

The new freeway in Ohio provided smooth, efficient travel as Phil, Fran, Tim, and I lazed in the cargo area. Papaw always drove like someone chased him, scaring his bride and daughter. Even Dad, occasionally a heavy foot, needed assurances that we'd make it in one piece.

"Willie, you're scarin' the Hell out of us and every other driver on the highway. Do you mind slowing down some? Jesus Christopher, we'd like to get there *alive and in one damn piece*!" Dad asked kindly.

"Look, I aim to get there, you know? Between Emily's hungry-sick ways and Jaybird suckin' in the wind, we'll take all day, and that ain't how I do it!" Papaw insisted.

Mom usually loved to stop often, which lent itself to accessible criticism. Papaw kept a coffee can in the car for "emergencies only," but none of us kids needed it. The man pressed on like he was getting paid by the mile.

The open freeways of Ohio ended when we hit Kentucky and landed on US 25. Besides going through every small town along the way, the hills and twists made Papaw slow down.

As the drive slowed our pace, with tractor-trailers unable to negotiate the curvy roads like passenger cars, we kids took to the coloring books and crayons. Passing cattle and hog farms soured the air for everyone, but one person put that to shame.

Mom and Mamaw calmed down considerably at the slower speeds we endured. Mamaw commented on the state of our terrible world, and Mom somehow agreed with the assessment. Then, from nowhere, Mamaw shrieked.

"Oh, oh, oh my God, Emily...you *stink*! Put that winder (Translation: window) down now! I swear I swollered it whole and if my breath smells like that, well, I will kill you- kill you dead! Great God Almighty!"

The kids ignorantly colored, not realizing the horror coming. Mom became an expert and originator of the term "silent-but-deadly," releasing a toxin the Environmental Protection Agency needed to investigate.

I could only see Mom's shoulders moving up and down, her head bobbing as she opened a window. Mamaw clambered for hers, cussing as she went.

"Durn, woman I raised you better than that! You got people trapped in a car! Ooh, I *can't* take it! It's enough to gag a buzzard, I tell you! She crapped her pants! Maybe she blew a durn hole in 'em! Lord have mercy!" Mamaw bellowed.

From the tailgate area, where we happily kept busy with crayons, we didn't know what seeped into our direction.

Phil waved his hand under his nose, being closest to the perpetrator. He looked over at Tim and pointed. Tim, for his part, kept coloring until it hit him squarely in the face.

"Phil, durn, you stink! Nasty, nasty cuss, that's you, Phillip! Oh, my Lord, it's awful!" Tim yelled.

Phil complained that he'd done nothing wrong. Fran got a whiff and waved both hands in her face before the awful scent hit me, too!

We were trapped with no place to go! Papaw closed the wagon's back window so we did not fall out before we left for the drive. The side windows didn't open, but all four kids screamed in unison!

"Hey, oh, open the back window, please!" We screamed. We collectively chose carbon monoxide poisoning or death over whatever Mom delivered to destroy us!

When Papaw reacted to all the noise coming behind him, he put the tailgate window down to get us breathable air. Neither he nor Dad knew what the rest of us were talking about as they sat up in front. As Mamaw asked how the stench made us run for cover, we panted for fresh air.

"Emily, Jesus, Mary, and Joseph! I'm glad we got these vent windows open. They saved Willie and me. Okay, so you sit and laugh at the rest of us. *Damn* those Brussels sprouts! I bet I never buy 'em again, betcha that!" Dad yelled to the crowd. Papaw drove on, and the air cleared later.

Roadside attractions were big, and our family could not get past Dogpatch Trading Post, close to London. With log cabins, teepees, and covered wagons posted on the grounds, it looked like Daniel Boone just left for the frontier.

Papaw pulled the family wagon in and parked. Before we exited the car, Mamaw gave the marching orders we were all expected to follow.

"Now don't nobody go in there thinkin' we got lotsa time to shop here! My mother waits for us just down the road. And you young'un's best not try buyin no tommyhawks, spears, harmonicas, or anything else to make a bunch of durn noise! Everybody got it. I see y'all shaking them heads, so I'll not rattle on!"

We all got it loud and clear. Phil crowed about not intending to comply, and I couldn't blame him. Folks crimped what little fun there was, but how could we get around that?

Coonskin caps, musket rifles, and arrowheads adorned Dogpatch walls. Mom collected keychains and eyeballed plenty to choose from. Dad walked around nervously, not impressed by the merchandise. A pack of plastic Indians, cowboys, and wagons pacified my kid brother and me. Dull? Sure, but it meant our heads might stay attached at Ma Smith's shack. Who knew that Daniel Boone's factory in Japan made all the goodies? The guy got around!

We pulled into Ma Smith's one-room tiny home about an hour later. Bathroom? It was an outhouse parked outside by the railroad tracks. Kitchen? It was inside and plopped on the back wall. Beds sat alongside the walls, with handmade quilts, furthest from windows.

I surveyed the place for my nemesis, ol' wrinkles-and-eyeballs herself, Ma Smith! Her face displayed more cracks than a Stefanow family reunion. She wore a bonnet on her head like an Amish matriarch. She scared the bejesus out of all kids, not just me.

The adults greeted one another with hugs and kisses. I pushed Phil, Tim, and Fran before me while I looked for an escape route. Mamaw reacted to my actions, grabbed me by my left ear, and promptly put me in front. My family excelled at profanity; I could only *think* "dammit" while standing front and center.

"Okay, young'un's, give Ma Smith some sugar!" Mamaw crowed to the lambs and led them to slaughter.

My folks offered no assistance as I stood there helpless. I froze up, like when someone gets a good close-up of Bigfoot in the woods! I got scared witless, but Ma Smith wanted her kisses!

Mamaw wasn't one for patience, especially with kids. If she gave a command, then it became *law* and obeyed. I whipped up excuses as I stood there.

"I...I, uh, been coughin' and feelin' sick since...we left Ohio. No, really...!" I muttered. I could do no better.

"Boy, you better shake your ass and get over to your great granny! All she wants is your sugar, durn you! Get movin'!" Mamaw said.

I shook in my Keds shoes as Mamaw held tightly to that left ear! At a whim, my developing wit came forward.

"If she wants *sugar*, then she can get it in the kitchen!" I blurted out, unaware I'd pissed off every adult in the room.

In milliseconds later, Mamaw spun my frozen body on the wooden floor. I left skid marks as I fell into a woman who smelled of an old coal stove, baked biscuits, and sweat.

Ma Smith's wrinkles brushed against my skin while her toothless mouth gobbled my cheeks. Her bony body crushed me as I held my breath. I closed my eyes, prayed, and stiffened like I'd met my Maker. When she let go, I sprinted out the front door and didn't look back!

The rest of the victims took their poison more efficiently than I did. Everyone except Phil. I peered in from the front porch and saw Phil's terror-filled eyes. He tried backing into his "sugar," turning his head and screaming, "Somebody...help! Oh my God! I can't *take* it! No...no...no, oh God!"

All of us kids gathered outside on the porch to assess our trauma. Fran got us laughing when she said she'd run away from home if it ever happened again. We needed to stay outside all day because we knew our departure would end similarly.

Aunt Odie arrived with my cousin Edith and her daughter Jackie. Nobody warned the youngster about Ma, and then Edith gave us a dire warning.

"Y'all don't go near that well out back, you hear. The devil lives down there and he gets a hankerin' for children, so nobody goes near it!"

Nobody wanted to hear Edith's revelation. We needed an adventure, Lucifer or not. Fran produced an idea.

"Hey, y'all, those railroad tracks have plenty of rocks! If we know the devil's in that well, let's bomb his ass and keep him down there!"

Fran, the oldest and wisest child, put out a plan. That dark entity gave mankind trouble since the beginning, so we'd give him a headache at the very least!

Jackie survived her great grandma's invasion of personal space, cheering up as Fran told her what we planned. All five of us aimed one at a time with our volleys after we collected them. The fun finally arrived!

It wasn't long before the noise of the plinking rocks alerted the adults. Cousin Edith stuck her head out the door to see what we were up to. We dummied up, of course.

Another car came into view. Mom's cousin Frank, his wife Pat, and their boy Wang pulled up while we scattered. Wang, a wild child of the nth degree (His actual name was Wayne), knew we messed up the moniker and loved it!

Wang and his folks went inside, so Fran led us to watch for his reaction to the lady with the roadmap face. He squirmed, twisted, and shouted, but his Dad kept a gorilla grip on his neck so that Ma got herself a face full. Wang didn't cry as he ran out, but we laughed at him anyways.

"Dammit, that ol' lady gripped me like the last pork chop at the dinner table! Jesus, when we leave I'm runnin' outta here! I should have stayed in the car!" Wang told us.

Who could disagree? We told him of our plan to rock Satan's world.

"Yeah, that jackass caused me enough trouble already! Still, I don't care if he comes up outta that well, I'd rather face him than Ma Smith any *damn* day!" Wang bragged, semi-shocking us with adult language.

Everyone laughed and agreed. The fun reinstituted. Phil and Wang were two sides of the same coin. Both were in the winner-take-all sweepstakes on the highway to Hell with no stop signs or speed limits to slow them down. They were rivals and peers, but Wang stood out on this day.

While the rest of us shot rocks one at a time at the crusty old well, Wang asked for a cease-fire. We obliged, and he gathered a t-shirt full of as many stones as he could carry. Wang looked around at the little house and dashed to the well. He furiously dumped his ammo onto ol' Beelzebub himself as he laughed hysterically. We chuckled along until Edith rocketed out the front door.

"Listen you all! That there's a dangerous well. I told you what's in there. Leave it *alone*!" Edith insisted.

Wang offered no respect for his older and wiser cousin. A budding potential man, he told Edith to take a hike.

"We ain't doin' nothing wrong here! We're just funnin' and we ain't scared one bit!" Wang replied.

Edith cussed under her breath but went back inside. She sought out more rank. Our futures were at stake when Mamaw showed up at the back door. She itched for a reason to plaster someone's behind.

"You stupid young'un's been warned, haven't you? Don't tell me Edith ain't told you all about that durn well! Unless y'all want striped britches, you better straighten up and fly right!" Mamaw commanded.

Our temporary fun ended. Even Wang appeared smart enough to avoid crossing Mamaw! The giant willow tree behind the house put fear in his rear.

Our visit ended, and the parents lined us up like criminals in a police lineup. I slipped in near the back, hoping the old woman wore herself out with everyone else by the time I arrived. I dug in my heels and rode the grooves into the mouth of the lion. Head down, eyes closed, my penance ended, but the trauma stuck around for decades.

Kentucky for the win

Chapter 8

Ma Smith ailed for decades. Frail and ancient but looking like a living Egyptian mummy, she terrified the fire out of me; I wanted no harm to befall her. Mamaw, the only sibling moving south for good, helped Papaw produce an acceptable plan.

Papaw came up five years short of his union pension. He could earn enough hours by working April-November in Ohio to qualify. In that case, he'd prepare easily and retire comfortably in his home state. My mom and Dad were thrilled and honored to have him stay with us for the short term while he wintered in Kentucky on his unemployment wages. Mamaw, never thrilled with the compromise, helped sister Odie in the care of the matriarch. Simple enough.

My mom's mental health became the wildcard nobody foresaw before the plan went into action. My family welcomed Papaw's calming, caring presence. Papaw got his own bedroom while Phil and I doubled up in mine. Everyone made sacrifices for the sake of Ma Smith.

Our routine at our Eastlake home altered, but it felt for the better. Papaw left early each morning and arrived by four in the afternoon, to the minute. Dad worked in a salary position, and we never knew when he'd return.

Papaw got in the door, washed up, grabbed a Stroh's beer, and poured one into a tumbler each afternoon. When the beer's head languished, he'd load it up with salt to create the odd mushroom-like effect I marveled at. On Papaw's payday Fridays, he'd get us Ponderosa steakhouse meals or buy Biagio's pizza as a treat! Each night at bedtime, he'd bounce around in his bed, scarf down his Di-Gel's tablets, and sleep soundly.

Papaw's few words carried weight. The neighborhood loved having him around, as evidenced by kids calling him "Papaw" like Phil and I did. One day, Robin Welch sat beside him on our glider couch.

"Uh, Papaw, how come you live here part of the year and the rest in Kentucky?" Robin inquired.

Papaw cocked his head, looked at Robin, and said:

"Robin, you've met my wife. Enough said!"

Robin keenly understood the inference and never asked again, but Papaw wanted things clear.

"My woman insists I'm up here steppin' out on her while she's raisin' our two young'uns, but the entire world knows better! I bust my ass, come home and then pray I make it until retirement."

Sometimes, Mamaw came up from Kentucky on a Greyhound bus to visit and, more likely, to try catching Papaw doing anything untoward. Bringing our aunt and uncle really livened up Alva Drive.

Mamaw made it clear one day that her family needed to visit her sister Ev in Windham, Ohio. Papaw complied with the hour-long drive while we stayed at home. They missed the latest excitement while out.

Hours later, Phil and I tossed a football back and forth on the street. Occasionally, it hit the overhead wires, causing reception interruption for the Slopstick family. The old man came out, cussed at us, and returned inside.

My little brother and I ignored them, just like we'd learned. Their oldest child, Peggy, bought a new Camaro and raced it out of their driveway while Phil and I escaped. Mom witnessed the entire scene, livid like never before!

Mom took stock of the inventory, ensuring both boys survived near-mangling by the teen driver. She marched us back home but vowed to make things right. She stomped over to see Penny Slopstick.

Mom barely got out our door as Penny left hers to complain about our disrespect for her television viewing habits. The inevitable collision came to Eastlake!

I watched from the front porch as both women stopped mere feet from the property lines, waving their arms and screaming at each other. I clearly heard Mom.

"Penny, your crazy daughter almost killed my young'un's today, and she will pay for it, you hear me?" Mom shouted.

"Emily, you're getting up in arms over nothing! She didn't come that close to them. Besides, those two brats always disrupt our antenna with their ball playing!" Penny answered.

Mom *loved* it when told to calm down. In Mom's medicated era, she could still be a wild child. Hands-on hips meant she'd not be tamed.

"Penny, if she kilt my kids, well, there'd not be a piece of her left when I got done! You'd find neither hide nor hair of that little one, I tell you!"

Penny couldn't let things go as Mom walked back into our house. Penny followed Mom across our yard and tapped Mom's shoulder while screaming about being ignored. A near-fatal move happened when she spun Mom around.

Without missing a beat, Mom's spin and her uppercut's momentum caught Penny under the chin. Penny's feet lifted upwards as she crashed to the turf! Phil and I rejoiced in the doorway. Mom became known as the short-heavyweight champ of the neighborhood- introducing...Emily "Fireplug" Stefanow!

When Penny came to, her husband helped her into their house. Then, the police arrived on our doorstep just as my grandparents returned home.

"Mrs. Stefanow, did you strike your neighbor here today?" The friendly officer asked.

"Durn right, I did, but you gotta hear the whole story!" Mom exclaimed.

Penny kept an icepack on her busted chin as she sat on her porch with her husband. They strained to catch every word.

"Well, ma'am, with all due respect, you cannot assault a neighbor and get away with it! That's not how the law works!" The cop said.

By this time, Mamaw stood beside Mom, looking skeptically at the situation. Papaw kept us kids inside and away from the melee.

"Look here, this woman came over, grabbed my shoulder, and spun me around. I defended myself, buddy!" Mom screamed.

Penny and her spouse leaped off the porch to dispute the claim. They wisely held their ground in their yard as they surveyed Mamaw's scowl. The cop put out his arms to divide the crowd and spoke loudly.

"Mrs. Slopstick, did you cross the property line and put your hands on Mrs. Stefanow? Yes, or no?"

"Well, now, she ignored me, and I needed her attention, so yes I did..." Penny said as the cop cut her off.

"Okay, so you did that. This discussion is over! I am not filling out a report for something so dumb! Both of you get back into your homes and stay there. Mrs. Slopstick, you're at fault here! I am going back to the station!" The cop said.

Penny never came close to the property line ever again. Mamaw screamed her threats, regardless.

"You better keep your ass on that side of the line, woman! 'Cuz if my girl don't break you into little pieces, then I will! You done stirred up a mess of trouble, little woman!" Mamaw threatened.

Things momentarily calmed down until Phil and I found a possum inside a sewer grate across the street from our house. Papaw seemed mildly interested, but Mamaw saw an easy meal waiting to be cooked.

Neighbors gathered to see the fuss. Mamaw claimed "finders-keepers" for the rodent. Nobody else considered the critter anything but live roadkill. Mamaw did not want to be denied.

"Young'un's, that is good meat right there! It's good eatin', I tell you! Junior get me a ball-bat, shovel or better yet...a pickax and I'll make him something out of this world! He'll supply us with meat like you ain't never seed!" Mamaw crowed.

Our citified neighbors got disgusted with the idea and tried changing her mind. Fat chance.

"Look, y'all, you ain't never been hungry, have you? Not one of you lived through a Dee-pression, that I know for shore! When you got no food, you'll not be so durn picky! This animal right here is durn good eatin'!" Mamaw insisted.

Mom ran inside, sick to her stomach with the thought. Papaw convinced Mamaw that being in the city made food a different commodity entirely. With tremendous pressure, she gave up on her gamey meal for something more civilized.

Cousin Wang and his folks, Frank and Pat, invited us to Akron for entertainment at the local Moose Club. Frank, a dues-paying member, had access to liquor, beer, cards, and pool tables. They loved Mamaw and Papaw dearly, so the group of us showed up.

Things were lively when Dad and Frank got together. Each had their pet name for the other. They played billiards, accused each other of cheating, and swore loudly. When the ladies left the hall to go shopping, the party began.

A handful of patrons hated having kids around the boys' club, as it was called. Phil and Wang, rivals extraordinaire, mercilessly traded jabs and insults like their fathers. When the heat turned up, things got out of control.

The bartender voiced his concerns to anyone listening.

"Look, you got two brats over there ruining the atmosphere! Keep 'em under control, or you'll have to go!"

Fran, Tim, and I kept a low profile on a miniature bowling machine so we knew what the man squawked about. Phil and Wang got unwanted attention, so Frank stepped in forcefully.

"Look, I got free rein in here, right? I mean, I do pay for this right every month! Our boys are only normal kids havin' fun!" Frank yelled. My Dad and grandfather nodded concurrently.

"Frank, you know, I wouldn't care, but someone is gonna get hurt, that's all!" The bartender complained.

Frank's Kentucky blood boiled over. He sorted things out.

"Hunky, our boys are same-sized, same-aged, and just as doggone ornery! With the wives out the way, let's let 'em go at it, you know, get this fightin' stuff out of their systems!"

Dad enthusiastically agreed. Papaw nodded his approval again. The boys were taken to a far corner of the club and given the tournament rules. Ah, the 1970s!

"You can scrap, you can punch anywhere but below the durned belt, and pound all you like! There's no bitin', no kickin', no spittin', and mostly no cryin'!" Frank explained.

The bout's maximum ten-minute length kept the father's ringside.

The bartender watched from afar but moved in quickly, for nobody wanted to hear his speech.

"Frank, I am warnin' you for the last time! If you keep this up, I'll call the cops if I must so they can stop this madness!"

"Looky here, man, me and Hunky already agreed to let these fellers get this outta their system. If you pick up that phone, you'll be pullin' it outta your ass when I get done with you!" Frank bellowed.

Dad and Papaw stood beside Frank in solidarity and defiance. The bartender shook his head, muttered to himself, and returned to the bar. What happened next shocked us all.

Grown men rose from their tables and placed cash on the bar! Phil and Wang wore different colored shirts, so the bettors divided as they felt fit.

"Hey, now, I want five dollars on that kid in the blue shirt!" Yelled one man. (Phil wore red.)

Others surmised that Wang looked meaner and placed cash on their pick. Papaw asked to keep track of the money but seemed uncomfortable doing it.

An audible "ding-ding" by Frank got the round going! Phil and Wang furiously threw wild punches at each other. All offense- no defense came to play, and the men cheered them on! Plenty of oohs and ahhs came from the pugilistic fans! The bout's honest-to-goodness, live-action rock 'em-sock 'em robots thrilled the attendees!

An even bout raged when I saw my grandfather secretly cheering Wang! What? At least I knew why he did it.

Phil pushed Papaw's buttons when he could. His spite work is legendary within our family. One day, he gave my little niece a plastic machine gun to bop Papaw's noggin as he napped on a hammock in our backyard. Poor Papaw shot up from his nap like someone with missiles up his rump!

Another day Papaw looked over his tools in the trunk of his car. He'd just gotten home to our house and was clearly weary from high summer temperatures. Phil and I tossed a baseball to each other innocently at first.

Phil smiled a devilish grin, and before I could think to stop the melee coming, he fired the ball at warp speed into Papaw's open trunk!

Papaw's whole head peered into his toolboxes as he rearranged things. He didn't see the rocket coming his way. The ball exploded on impact in the trunk, bouncing pinball-like as the old man smashed his head on the trunk lid!

"Damn you, Phillip! Doggone you to Hell and back. Come here you little heathen. Get over here! You are not gonna live to see another day! Great God Almighty!" Papaw screamed!

Phil took off like a jackrabbit, hopping fences and disappearing where no one could find him. These instances and many others factored into why Wang became Papaw's ally in the fight!

The pummeling continued but ended in a draw when both pre-teen boys quit. The show ended with bloody faces, handshakes, and a round of root beer just as the ladies returned. All three women were enraged!

"Jesus, Mary and Joseph, Gusty, what happened in here? These boys look like they beat themselves silly!" Mom screamed.

Dad, always the negotiator, tried making up a lie with his buddy Frank, but both men stuttered in surprise.

"Frank Smith, you idiot, why is Wayne's face so red? Why the Hell is he so sweaty? Good Lord, look at Phillip, too! Ignorant men! I swear, these fools can't be trusted, ladies!" Pat said in anger.

Papaw, ever the silent partner in life, did not escape either. Mamaw bucked up against him and began the interrogation.

"Willie, what in tarnation you been a doin' to these little fellas? Reminds me all the world of a cockfight back in the durned hills! Ain't you men got no more brains than to let these kids kill each other? Boy, I tell you, this she-it happens every time you leave a man in charge! Yep, every damn time men get together in a place like this, they lose whatever little brains the Good Lord give em!" Mamaw surmised.

The ladies missed the payout with the bartender, and Papaw settled before the women stepped inside. I didn't know who set the odds or made money, but plenty of men left happy that day. I know of three unsatisfied grown men; their long rides home were the penance they paid.

As the five years Papaw lived with us ended, I felt sad about his Kentucky situation. It wasn't like Mom stopped visiting, but Papaw's emotional, physical, and mental health dropped after his departure.

On a bright sunny morning, my parents took us to the Bluegrass State again. We arrived after traveling all day and got refreshed by the following morning. Papaw surprised us, kids.

"Young'un's let's git 'er going to the park for the day! Take your playthings and let's go!" Papaw insisted.

Fun existed just around the corner. We took off in Papaw's big Buick for a state park. On the way into it, Papaw pulled over, stopped, opened his trunk, and removed his police revolver.

Bang...bang... boom went the sound as it echoed throughout the park. An unfortunate rattlesnake didn't make it across the road. Papaw put the weapon away, and we found a picnic spot.

"Willie, I swear, you ain't never tried gettin' me to drive one of your vehicles! You never gimme the chance! Why I bet I could drive better than you with just a little bit of practice. I could!" Mamaw said.

Papaw ignored the request for decades. Mamaw wore him down, so he relented, and we all got back into the car. Mamaw did okay at first.

Tree-lined lanes passed by slowly as Mamaw got more confident behind the wheel. She almost killed us when Papaw told her to pull up to a barrier made from downed trees!

While Mamaw mastered cornering, maneuvering, and lane-changing, her braking left much to be desired. We reached the top of a scenic overlook Papaw wanted us to see. He told her calmly to roll up and stop. When that didn't work, he became more animated than at any time I'd ever seen.

"Jay...Jay...Jaybird, durn it, Jemima, hit the brakes...now! Mash that brake pedal, dammit! Hit the dad-gummed brakes!" Papaw screamed.

The front bumper smacked the log and rolled onto it, scraping everything underneath. Papaw leaped out and made us do the same!

"Willie Smallwood, durn you, don't you ever talk to me like that again, you understand me? Stupid, stupid man! I ain't no damned child you can bark at any time you feel like it. Understand?" Mamaw barked while sitting calmly behind the wheel.

Papaw took us in a group and let us peer over the edge of a one-hundred-foot drop-off below! He shook his head and spoke.

"Bunt, you coulda kilt us all down there, you see that? Never again do you get behind the wheel of any car long as I am alive." Papaw said.

Mamaw grunted, took a quick look down, and shook her head as if to say, "Well, yeah, Willie, it's close, but not that close!" End of discussion. At least the picnic safely came and went.

On the drive home, Papaw looked closely at Phil and me for hair length. He asked when we'd gotten our last haircut. Like an idiot, I spoke up.

"Papaw, we don't need haircuts like you do. We live in the Big City and men wear longer hair nowadays!" I boasted.

My granddad, a traditionalist in the purest sense, saw no grey areas or place of compromise. He spoke up just before Mamaw did.

"Morphydites! Morphydites, dammit! You boys won't skip haircuts down here! I am takin' you to Dub's barber shop so's he can make you proper! Or...I can take you out back of the barn and turn you from rooster to hen with my knife! What you prefer?"

Mamaw snickered, then openly laughed as she mocked us.

"You fellers ain't got much use fer that piece of skin now, but one day you'll want to use it. Your Papaw is right! Haircuts or... you'll squat to pee the rest of your days! We'll hear no more squawkin', right?"

Wide-eyed and scared, even Phil agreed with my answer.

"Okay, then, it's haircuts like you say, Papaw! Uh, we'd like to leave Kentucky with what we came here with!" I said with enthusiasm. We picked up Mom and Dad before cruising to the barbershop.

Dub's old-timey shop, complete with outdated magazines such as "Farm Life," "Better Homes and Gardens," and "Country Songs and Stars," displayed dust and cigarette/cigar smoke. Dub stood six feet, six inches tall and exhibited well over four hundred pounds of blubber. His sweaty left hand clamped itself over my head to keep it still. At the same time, the right worked feverishly with scissors and clippers interchangeably.

Dub's stories of current events, civil rights, and the communist menace were over the heads of the kids, but he relished telling his opinion. His fat, greasy fingers blinded my eyes as he chipped away. I went in working on the John Denver look and came out of the chair as a Marine recruit. I likely lost a decade of style. Yippee.

Uncle Tim sat through his initiation without a word, knowing escape was futile. Phil held the last hope for our generation.

Dub breezed through with Tim and me with no problems. Phil enjoyed hyperactivity before its elevated status arrived. Even medications worked iffy. He squirmed, cried, and twisted for the next fifteen minutes. Papaw paid the man, and we went back to their place. The five-minute ride home kept Phil cackling the whole way. We told him to "man up" and shut up!

Back at my grandparent's homestead, Phil continued protesting. He showed Mom the back of his head, and she gasped!

"Jesus, Mom, Phil's head is bleedin' bad! Dub clipped his ear, too! Damn him!" Mom screamed.

Mamaw went into action as the rest of us watched. She grabbed the phone with no mercy in her countenance.

"Dub, Dub, you big stupid e-dit! Why you durned tub o' lard! You cut my grandson's ear! He's a bleedin' you dumbass!" Mamaw barked.

"Now Jaybird, I uh, well, I told that littlest boy to hold still, or I'd cut him! You heard me tell him!" Dub yelled back.

"Listen to me, you lard-ass sumbitch! I got my own weapons, and I'll come down there, cut you into a million pieces and slop the hogs with what's left of you! That's *if* they'd eat you! Big. Stupid. E-dit!" Mamaw threatened.

By this time, Papaw wrestled the phone from his bride and hung up. He agreed with her in principle but not in technique.

"Bunt, you done said enough. Show some charity- we known Dub since birth!"

"Willie Smallwood, durn your hide! You better never lay hands on me like that again or you'll be in your grave before sundown! And I *did* show that big, dumb e-dit charity! I'd do to him what he *done* to us! Wouldn't cost him a dime for eye for eye, tooth for tooth, and cut for cut! You know Phillip may be a demon, but he's still our grandson! Dub ain't gonna get away with cutting our kin, Willie!" Mamaw screeched.

From that day forward, we went to another shop for mandatory Kentucky haircuts when we visited. Dub lost out on his chance to try Mamaw's quick weight-loss plan!

Neighbor, Ms. Carnes, housed prize rabbits that won yearly awards at the county fair. They were valued for whatever distinguishes one rabbit from the next. My grandparents offered no opinion, but George, their playful German shepherd pup, developed a taste for them that he couldn't resist.

While we'd all been out one night, ol' George busted out of the pen, hopped the fence into Mrs. Carnes's yard, and picked out a tasty meal. Papaw pulled his Ford F-100 into the driveway, and even in the dark, we saw the carnage.

"Jesus, Lord, that dog will be the end of us, Jaybird!" Papaw cried.

"Doggone him, Willie, he's more trouble than he's worth! We get him to keep the fox outta the hen house, but he ends up eatin' rabbits instead! Durn his hide! I'll brain him good! He's an e-dit, too!" Mamaw promised.

Mom made her beeline into the house, dodging entrails as Jim Brown used to avoid tacklers. Yes, the "eck...eck...eck" sound made us boys laugh as Mom zipped into the house.

Mamaw told Tim to clean up after his dog and hide the incriminating remains. The smile left his face immediately.

"Mommy...mommy...I ain't got no gloves or nothin'! I can't pick that up, mommy!" Tim yelled.

Mamaw's commands were distinct from suggestions. When she spoke, people moved *or* paid the price.

"Durn you, Timmy Smallwood, I said you get a move-on, wrap up that crap in the driveway and toss it over yonder in that pond so's nobody sees it! Them people will be home soon! Now get!" Mamaw insisted.

Papaw shook his head and went inside to check on Mom. Fran took off before Mamaw could shift the job to her. The rest of us stood there numbly, not knowing how to help.

"Mommy...mommy...I ain't got no gloves or nothin'! I *can't* pick it up, mommy! Why there's blood, guts, and fur *everywhere*! No, I just can't!" Tim yelled again as he backed away from my irritated granny.

However, Tim didn't move fast enough, and Mamaw cracked him about his head and shoulders. He danced away, insisting he couldn't be the man for the job. Phil and I were frozen in our tracks as the drama unfolded. No way did we want to be drafted next!

"Timmy...Timmy...get that rabbit!" Mamaw shouted.

Tim twisted and writhed away from his angry mother, still insisting on gloves.

"Timmy...Timmy, damn you,...get *that* rabbit!" Mamaw shouted.

Mamaw smacked away at Tim's body while screaming her brains out. Dad stepped in to save the day.

"Here, here, dammit! Let that boy go, Jaybird! I'll get rid of that stupid rabbit! Jesus, Mary, and Joseph what a crazy family! Why me, Lord, how did I get involved with this bunch? Oh, Hellfire!" Dad said.

Phil and I watched from the covered porch, primarily out of eyesight from an angry grandmother intent on annihilating someone or something. We chased Tim as he ran inside to Papaw.

Dad, barehanded and cussing loudly, scooped up the remains of the prize animal, ran across the street, and threw everything into the swampy, reed-filled pond. The deed done; we slipped inside.

The next day, we awoke to Mamaw's traditional early morning breakfast. It smelled amazing, but gee, the world showed freaking darkness outside. She didn't care that the rest of the world had no intent to be farmers.

I uselessly protested when she rolled us boys out of bed. With school out, why get up so early?

"Young'un, do you want to eat today? Huh? Well, if so, then you'll eat it when it's put in front of you! This house ain't no restaurant or dad-blamed roadside café! Shake a leg or lose one!" Mamaw said.

Freshly baked biscuits were hard to resist. Mamaw's homemade butter was added to the bargain. Several pounds of bacon stacked a foot high awaited the gang. Mamaw's famous "floating" eggs I *could* resist! They floated because of the multiple scoops of lard she fried them in. An industrial-sized lard container sat beside the stove.

The eggs turned my stomach, so I avoided them. Mamaw noticed and planted three eggs onto my plate as I objected. Mom shot me the "uh-uh" grunt, and I complied. One by one, I took the eggs off my plate, turned them sideways to let the grease drip onto a napkin, and then consumed them without asking questions. It's a wonder any of us lived past forty years when cholesterol is factored in.

Up and around without much to do allowed Phil, Tim, and I to explore the property outside. Mamaw insisted we stay off the ladder that led to rooftop storage. She didn't want us rummaging through anything. It seemed simple enough.

Phil "poked the bear" with our saintly grandmother, his idea ignorant and deadly. They'd reached a sort of détente after Phil's numerous near-death exterminations by my grandparents. An uneasy truce did not last.

Phil unwisely climbed the ladder to find the forbidden fruit he later regretted. With an idea of any kind in his skull, nobody could stop him. He blatantly disobeyed while Tim and I watched his insubordination.

Slowly, Phil crept up the fifteen-foot ladder with no fear of heights. At the top, he reached for a door that led into attic storage. Upon opening it, he got his just reward.

A wasp nest with hundreds of angry tenants met Phil head-on. He didn't bother trying to close the door while scurrying down the ladder, more aware of the height he'd ascended in his ignorance.

He jumped off about three feet from the ground, screaming and swearing. He rolled around in the grass as I nervously laughed from the cornfield fifty yards away. Mom ran out the back door to investigate with Mamaw in hot pursuit.

"Jesus, Phillip, there's bees everywhere!" Mom said, swatting and trying to rescue him. Mamaw stepped back to the house and chuckled.

"Well, young'un, what did your Mamaw tell you? You don't listen to no one, bud, and got your medicine for it! Haha. You know, them wasps got the worse end of the deal! They got a bite of your flesh, and you know they're gonna die! Hehehehe! Yep, those wasps will die for shore! Hahaha!" Mamaw said with glee.

Mom got Phil inside and found that he'd been stung twenty-seven times. Dad and Papaw just shook their heads while Mom stewed at Mamaw for days after. Mamaw's lack of empathy did not help the situation.

"Emily, now you know that child's plumb full of wickedness, right? He's a mean one, for shore! You baby him too much and it ain't right! He minds nobody even when you warn him for his own good! He's gonna get the law on him one day and then what'll happen?" Mamaw bragged.

The perpetual struggle of comparing parenting skills became infinite with the mother-daughter duo. Neither could agree on discipline, and they argued about it frequently.

My parents and grandfather took a ride one night, leaving the rest of us at the house. With no kids allowed, I suspected they went on a "moon-run," meaning getting moonshine from a covert source. I walked the straight and narrow pathway with Mamaw unsupervised and unfettered in her authority. One teen lady chose something entirely different.

"Fran, Frances, get to peelin' them taters for supper tonight. Did you hear me, little lady? Get a move on so's we can eat soon! Got me? Mamaw barked.

Fran either ignored her mother or willingly defied her. Regardless, no repentance existed.

"Frances, Frances! Get to them taters like I told you! Move along!" Mamaw shouted.

Phil, Tim, and I saw the storm brewing. Mamaw clarified earlier that we'd be shucking corn, snapping peas and beans if we wanted a meal. We three kept our mouths shut, perhaps because we were hungry. We sat with Mamaw in the living room, watching a Western movie.

Moments passed before Mamaw craned her neck to see activity in the kitchen behind her. To her dismay, Fran became missing in action.

"Hey, now, little missy, jest what did I tell you 'bout them taters? If I must get up, you'll be one sorry filly, you know that?" Mamaw bellowed.

The atmosphere in the house changed. With fans running full force, swirling the oppressive heat around us, a chill entered our presence. Out of nowhere, a large potato sailed from the kitchen as if it possibly launched from Cape Canaveral! It instantly destroyed the lamp beside Mamaw, popping loudly and sending glass shards everywhere. The four horsemen of the Apocalypse rode into view!

The room darkened as Mamaw rose from her chair by an unseen force! She levitated while smoke poured from beneath her like a Kiss concert. She looked like an animated Disney villain, bringing the powers of Hell into her near-sacred living room! For once, it was not us boys acting up.

We, boys, were too alarmed to speak or breathe. Mamaw spun around, grabbed a rubber hose, and approached the kitchen.

"Why, you rotten piece of Hell! I'll get a hold of you, and there won't be nothin' left! I took you from the gutter, durn you, and gave you a place to live when nobody else gave a hot damn! This is the thanks we get for taking you in. No way!" Mamaw shrieked.

Fran vanished, and we sat in disbelief! Mamaw pointed toward the pile of potatoes on her kitchen table. Without a peep, we peeled better than Betty Crocker! Mamaw ruled the roost. Fran's execution had to wait.

Dad always said that Papaw deserved sainthood just for being married to Mamaw. His endurance is legendary, and his heart overflowed with love. His routine after retirement made an active man very sedentary. It may have been his way of saying goodbye.

Papaw suffered the first of several heart attacks months after our last family visit. The local hospital had no amenities, so there were successive ambulance rides to Lexington's University of Kentucky's Medical Center.

Combined with chain smoking, coal mining in Papaw's youth put him out of this world and into the next at an early age. How the family coped with the loss provided conjecture, but Mamaw marched on alone or not. The matriarch, newly single again, contemplated her future.

Smallwood kennel and farms Chapter 9

Papaw's passing left a void nobody filled for Mamaw. He retired in 1976 and lost interest in living. His zeal for life was utterly sapped. Mamaw's frustration and moodiness imposed themselves on the remaining population. Her "switch" significantly affected any soul unlucky enough to be in the target range. She preferred one about six feet long to swat unruly kids from any angle. She never missed!

Mamaw eventually replaced the tree branch with a rubber hose that East German prison guards probably endorsed. She used the hose or switch interchangeably as the mood took her. Our family believes she received training or stumbled upon the hose weapon later. After many beatings the day before, the hose left no marks the next day! No school calls about abuse like the tree branch always left. Mamaw didn't have YouTube videos to watch and no internet to gain knowledge. Who trained her, the CIA? We watched out and tried to pay attention! The Kentucky copperhead struck as needed!

With only one parent left, Mom packed us up and took us "down home," as she called it, at least quarterly. We were given no choice in the matter.

Mamaw's cranky moods were done no favors with Papaw gone. As her sounding board, he perfected it as people do. He'd mumble, nod, and pretend he cared or listened. Many thought he sounded like Paw from the "Hillbilly Bears" Hanna Barbera cartoons when he spoke. Quiet thunder, as one person called it. Now gone, no one took his place. Mamaw's patience wore thinner than ever.

My brother Phil found ways to push people's buttons that the poor souls didn't even acknowledge were in them. Mamaw became his prime target when he hated going to what he called "Mayberry- without the fun, Gus!" I agreed to a point, but until my release at eighteen, I sucked it up like the trustee I'd become. "Grin and bear it," as Mom taught us.

Uncle Tim and I carried a little cash from mowing yards all summer. We wanted a short adventure to the general store, up and over the hill to downtown London. Phil couldn't wait to tag along, getting his money from my folks. (He was just too young to earn any.) Mamaw gave our marching orders.

"Y'all don't get no squirty-guns, caps for them toy pistols, or anything that can break a winder 'round here, you hear me? Three boys had better pay attention or else I can see into the future where there's pain all around! Everybody got it?" Mamaw ordered.

We nodded that we understood, but "Shazam," I thought, what could we have fun with? Even a rubber baseball might break a window! Her rules meant that the lawn darts (Or Jarts to some of us) couldn't pass muster either! Daily ninety-five, hot, humid, life-sucking degrees met us outside, and the house had no air conditioning. We left with defiance in our hearts, hoping my folks could keep Mamaw busy instead of keeping the "all-seeing" eye upon us!

Just up the hill, we encountered barbed wire around a cattle pasture. We negotiated it with relative ease, dodging cow patties and ruts made by the heavy animals. We didn't anticipate a bull watching his flock, but we turned on the speed to get away from him. Thankfully, the bull did not see a reason to crush us.

The general store enticed us with golden doubloons filled with chocolate, army soldiers complete with parachutes, and three guns to blast ourselves with water. Dumb.

We avoided the cattle on the return trip but walked a dangerous stretch of curved road wooded on both sides. We avoided any fatalities there, taking our luck with Mamaw. More ignorance.

Mom and Dad weren't around when we got back. They'd left to pick Frances up from work. What could go wrong if we stayed *outside* and away from Mamaw? We justified our disobedience with childish logic.

Mamaw worked the laundry in the back of the house while we shot each other gleefully in the heat. The slow outside water faucet made us refill our weapons inside.

Phil and Tim carefully took care of theirs while I played lookout outside the bathroom door. Mamaw sat in the living room to watch "rasslin" (Translation: wrestling). It occupied my granny's whole being. The two boys scrambled out the back door to hide outside. I went to the bath sink and refilled my gun. I didn't see Mamaw take laundry and put it into a basket. The other guys did.

As I stepped from the room, the screen door opened to Mamaw's back. My kid brother and my favorite uncle unleashed both barrels of water...through the screen and onto my granny. She yelled, turned around, and saw me standing there. The other two eggheads split the scene, running out into the cornfield to hide.

Mamaw placed her weapons around the house to "stripe asses with," as she named it, but I wasn't sure if she'd holstered one and drawn on me. It didn't matter at all. I faced judgment from an angry goddess.

"You little *heathen*! I am goin' to skin you alive, you natty-assed young'un! Don't you try runnin' from me! Come back here, boy!" Mamaw screamed.

I stood in place and ran as fast as possible, getting nowhere! I faced Godzilla, Dracula, and a demon all at once. She swung her switch with reckless abandon as I struggled to move. Zorro would have indeed been proud of how Mamaw wielded her weapon! I tried getting out the screen door, but those other guys found a way to lock it.

I screamed as I tried pulling the door off its hinges to get out. Mamaw muttered something in other tongues as she swung for the fences.

"Hush, hush, I say...hush! Your durned cryin' ain't gonna save yer ass now! When I get a hold of you, there ain't no escape! Do you hear me? Boy, I said to hush that mouth and take yer medicine!" She bellowed.

Forty-seven licks later, my legs and back resembled a New York City roadmap. The blood crept down my legs into my socks before she quit. She let me go because she zipped straight out the front door, around the house, and into the cornfield. And at that point, I did not care one bit! She hunted for fresh game like one on safari.

I nursed my wounds in the bathroom, dabbing the backs of my legs with toilet paper. The welts were everywhere. My folk's outrage would bubble up, but we boys were at fault. Minor infractions received significant consequences in Mamaw's domain.

Phil disappeared like Houdini, but Tim could not be so fortunate. Getting bigger and taller than his nephews meant he needed to be better at camouflage, and...he wasn't! Mamaw lit him up like a downtown Christmas tree. I heard screams emanating from the cornfield and nodded in agreement. They were getting their own! My view from the backyard would have been great on film.

"Timmy, I told you all no squirty guns, and you got 'em anyway! You'll learn to mind me when I say somethin' you big stupid e-dit! I will make sure you never forget that when I make a promise, I keep it!" Mamaw yelled while striking Tim furiously.

Tim tried running, but for an old lady, Mamaw kept up with him! She lashed out at Tim, damaging the cornstalks as she swung wildly as in a hillbilly rodeo. When Mamaw tired, she yelled for Phil to get his due. Jesus could not have coaxed him out.

"Phillip, I will find you; you know I will! And when I do, you're gettin' double what these two got! If I gotta chase your ass, I'm gonna wear it out! You hear me, boy? Y'all don't wanna mind me and you'll pay the price, that I guarantee!"

Phil's hiding place he kept secret. My kid brother could not be dumb! He held his position and prayed for our parents to come back.

Mamaw told Tim and me to wash up since dinner preparations were starting, and we'd help if we wanted to eat. Neither of us negotiated anything. We snapped peas, shucked corn, and peeled potatoes while Mamaw kept a sentry duty lookout for Phil.

My sibling held out before sneaking around to the front door. Dogs barked, and a rooster crowed as Phil came inside. Unbelievably, he calmly sat in the living room as if he were immune to the shellacking Tim and I took.

"Well, lordy, I told you, durn it! I am gonna roast your ass like you ain't never had! Get over here, you lil dummy! You will learn to mind me if it's the last damned thing I do on God's green earth!" Mamaw screamed as she dashed into the living room.

Phil took off, and Mamaw gave chase. Lamps were toppled, and furniture leaped by both. Tom and Jerry, Bugs Bunny, and Elmer Fudd were outdone in the live cartoon playing out in our midst. Tim and I dared not laugh or snicker because Mamaw's stop-sign red face came into view.

Mamaw went behind the couch as Phil slipped over it. She latched on like he was her last meal. Phil lay there helpless, or so we thought. Mamaw scanned the room for her stash of handy branches but couldn't find one.

As Mamaw leaned over Phil, calling him everything but a white boy, he tipped his head back and...spit right in her face! I saw blasphemy and the unforgivable sin live and in person. Phil planned to *die*!

Stunned, Mamaw stepped back to get a better grip and wipe the saliva from her face. Phil took his arm back and ran from the couch as if on fire! He climbed over a half-wall room divider, scattering its contents over the floor. I saw smoke coming from his shoes as he stormed out the door, over shrubs and a picket fence, howling into the woods across the street.

I dropped my potato peeler in the excitement and went to the back door, unlatched it quickly, and laughed while hiding behind the chicken coop. Tim stayed at his post while Mamaw called down Hellfire and brimstone on her abominable grandson.

"That child, that child ain't nothin' but that Satan himself, you hear me? He'll be laid out when I get my hands on him. No, he'll be laid to rest! That's what'll happen! He is gonna meet his Maker today! And there ain't one soul that can stop me!" Mamaw screamed.

I composed myself before I went inside. Mamaw rocked furiously in her chair. Tim and I finished, then kept out of sight.

My parents drove up with Fran and came inside. Mamaw's eyes glowed fire as she told them what had happened.

"That boy is gonna die! I get these hands on him and there won't be enough of him left to fill a cee-gar box! He's evil, I tell you! He needs to be snuffed out, and I am just the one to do it!"

My baby brother pushed boundaries like no one else. Both parents disciplined him quickly enough, but it was his termination if Mamaw got her way.

Mom spoke up first.

"Mom, we know how you beat folks when you get the chance, but we'll be doing the spankin' on Phil. We'll make sure he never does this again, we promise."

The justice complex inside my grandmother meant no compromise. Her mind could not be swayed. Phil answered *her* only!

"Seein' how doggone stupid he acts tells me your actions ain't doin' enough to stop this boy! He keeps up and he's gonna end up in prison someplace, mark my words. Well, he's got Hell to pay when he comes back in. I'll fry him like he ain't never seed! Why it'll look like Cherokee smoke signals in the dad-blamed sky when I let up!" Mamaw boldly proclaimed.

Dad stepped in before Mom could speak (A genuine rarity) and pledged to take care of Phil's offense in his own way. The speech went down as a wool biscuit sticking in Mamaw's craw. She'd have the last word.

"Gus, I will have that boy's head on a platter if I choose, do you understand me? He spit in my face after buyin' them guns I told them not to! No, I will stripe him like a barber's pole, I sure will!" Mamaw gloated.

"Well, Jaybird, then get to it, and start with me!" Dad said.

Mamaw could not be moved by Dad's suggestion, which only inflamed the volatile standoff.

"Look, I know what he did was wrong, but you will not use those treetops you use on your kids, okay? You don't know when to stop! You stand over your kids beating the shit out of them while you tell them to hush! Nobody is gonna beat my kids like that!" Dad insisted while Mom tag-teamed him to jump back into the melee.

"Mom, we know how you draw the durned blood! I know it better than anyone! You think I've forgotten one lick from your hand, belt, or switch? No, Gusty is right! We'll take care of Phillip; just wait and see!"

"I see two e-dits in front of me who would not know how to discipline a young'un if it hit 'em in the face! I am gonna make him pay if I must drop you two like wild turkeys in the woods! I got my guns for a reason, you know that!" Mamaw said with relative ease.

"Well, Jemima, then you better get 'em! That's all I have to say! If the shootin' starts, then you better try me first!" Dad yelled.

Tim, Fran, Mom, and I could not believe what we heard. "High Noon" arrived in London, Kentucky, and it wasn't funny or pretty. We clearly outstayed our welcome.

Mom started packing, unable to bear Mamaw's threats. Her only comment came as she passed Mamaw's chair.

"Mom, you know when you go for them guns, you gonna have to kill us both, right? And if we grab 'em first, we gonna blast you to kingdom come! You think about that!"

The tense situation slowly came to a boil. Mamaw could've wiped out an entire village that day and slept soundly. We packed the car, drove away, and found Phil, scared and hungry, in a grove of evergreen trees across the street. My kid brother was alive but didn't get any of the potatoes I peeled, corn I shucked, or peas I snapped. Life is all about compromise.

Mamaw kept a running feud with most of the neighbors. The lady next door, Ms. Carnes, was labeled "Old Camelback" due to osteoporosis the elderly woman suffered from. Mamaw called her a busybody who kept her nose in everyone's business but hers. Ms. Carnes's son, named Geno, kept eyes on Fran. Still, that romance never happened under my granny's watchful, all-seeing eyes. No way.

Geno worked hard but had ten years of age ahead of Fran. That rankled Mamaw like a burr under her saddle. She saw no good side of Geno, even calling him "useless as teats on a bore hog, that boy!" The fireworks began when the boy's mother came to plead his case.

"Jaybird, now Geno ain't had no easy road in life, but he's got a good job with the county, and he can give Fran the things she needs!" Ms. Carnes said.

Mamaw wanted no part of matchmaking with anyone. With Papaw barely cold in the grave, the chores needed to be done to make the house function.

"Listen, here, Ms. Carnes, you talkin' stupid! Fran ain't got interest one in that useless, no-account boy of yours. You know, I declare, you put the ding in dingbat, lady! I swear, there ain't no use in carryin' on this crazy talk!" Mamaw bellowed.

Ms. Carnes knew no love was lost between the families. She thought of Willie as the only one to offer a kind word occasionally. She did not care what Jemima thought of her.

"Say what you will, Jaybird, but I think the young'un's decide for themselves who they court and who they don't! I reckon I better get outta here, I 'spose!" Ms. Carnes said.

"Yeah, see you can make a good decision, woman. And don't do any more visitin' if this is all you wanna talk about! She-it, too much done been said already!" Mamaw insisted.

While my Dad couldn't bring himself to wander to Kentucky every time we went, Mom kept Phil and me on a short leash for the obligatory trips. On this occasion, she even allowed Robin Welch along. He'd heard all the stories and expected the time of his life.

We arrived in London, and the house seemed bare without Papaw hanging around. His levity broke up the monotony, and he kept Mamaw on her toes. Mom's edginess spiraled without Papaw's presence. We boys stayed outside and kept ourselves busy. Sort of.

Tim showed Robin around the mini farm. The hogs, chickens, and endless garden made the city boy anxious, but Robin hid it well. Tim put out an idea to break up the dullness of everyday living.

"Boys, have you ever heard of Oscar Braun? Well, he's this old coot who lives over yonder in a haunted house, I swear! Let it get a little darker and we'll sneak up on him!"

We had no other plans for Robin, Phil, and me. Crickets, bullfrogs, and hound dogs were all we ever heard at night in London. We waited and followed Tim over a split-rail fence to Oscar's converted barn. At least the place *looked* haunted.

We had great fun creeping around outside. A functioning outhouse provided good cover while we did our survey. At the back of the house, we took turns two at a time to peek in on the old codger. He looked ancient to us.

We'd found an honest-to-goodness hillbilly Mister Magoo! His glasses were thicker than Coke bottles, and he bumbled through his house. Tim and I watched as he took a bottle of rubbing alcohol out, set it on the kitchen table, and added lemon juice. The man created his cocktail as we watched! He needed a little blood in his liquor stream, to be honest.

Phil and Robin changed places with us, peering in to see the same thing. Phil, naturally, began to snicker, meaning Robin did too. The old man looked around, grabbed a newspaper, and headed to the back door!

We ran fast, leaped the fence, and ducked for cover. The old guy tucked his paper under his arm, stepped into the outhouse, and continued his business.

Tim motioned for us to follow him back to his house. When there, he explained how the county just placed perfect throwing rocks on the road out front. Target acquired and bombs away!

Our volleys made a hellacious noise when striking the corrugated steel outhouse. The wooden roof proved okay but not as loud. Regardless, the cussing from the old man made us laugh harder with each strike at his privacy.

One outburst of several rounds of "ammo" slammed into the makeshift restroom. Mr. Braun's anger took front and center stage!

"Why whoever you is, I am gonna finish in here, come out and blast your brains to kingdom come! I still got my forty-five from the war and I know how to be usin' it, durn you to Hell!"

We cried with laughter, but the gun caught our attention swiftly. Even Robin wasn't taking chances.

"Timmy, you never said the old goat kept a weapon! I didn't come here to die! Let's get our butts in the house, fellas!"

Tim decided to call it a night so we could live to fight again.

"Boys, even if that ol' pecker had a gun, well, how in the Hell could he see us to shoot, huh? He can't find his behind with both hands, I tell you!" Tim bragged.

Our little fun ended, and we went inside. Mom and Mamaw lamented about the bad old days. Mamaw made it clear we boys needed to go to bed.

Phil and Tim shared one bedroom at the back of the house while Robin and I got the room in the front. Poor Fran got the couch when she got home. Mom and Mamaw took the master where the firearms hung on the wall.

Moments into bedtime, Phil and Tim scuffled about pillows or some such idiotic thing. Mamaw laid down the law, and they calmed down. Robin and I whispered.

"Dude, you think this place is haunted. I mean, look around the neighborhood! We're in some kinda holler, you know? Good place for a chainsaw massacre, get my drift? Seems like a 'Night of the Living Dead' place to me! Hell, this area scares me in the *daytime*, Junior!" Robin snickered.

"Man, the place creeps everyone out except Mamaw! She's scarier than anything we can dream up! I try not to think about it." I said politely.

We lay there on a fall night, talking about neighborhood girls, cars, and music. Robin looked across the room at a mysterious light above the dresser that swayed without any breeze. Terrified, he seemed out of sorts to me.

"Dude, this ain't nothin' paranormal! Go to sleep, tough guy!" I said to my macho friend.

"Junior, I tell you, something's goin' on here! I can't find my crucifix... it's gone! It sat on the nightstand, I swear!" Robin said as he panicked, and his voice went higher than usual.

The mystery light fascinated him, and as his terror ramped up, mine joined in! Someone had to be outside trying to scare us. Phil and Tim were suspiciously quiet. I hopped from the bed and went to their room, but they were discussing whether to marry Farrah Fawcett, Linda Carter, or Stevie Nicks. Duh. Teenage dreamers.

I re-entered the room, and Robin's sweat-soaked face glistened in the dark. Again, he needed his crucifix. Mamaw's ire or not, I flipped on the bedroom light long enough to find it on the dresser...under the haunted light! Robin openly prayed for my safety as I dashed over, grabbed Jesus for him, shut the light off, and jumped into bed before any adult noticed.

A few prayers later, he felt much better, but the light did not go away. We lay there in wonder when a crash from the front door sent us ducking under covers! We laughed when we realized our burglar called Mom let Fran in after she got off work. We eventually slept.

We woke the following day to Mamaw making the farmer's breakfast she'd made for decades. Just after daybreak, the smells overcame our slumber.

Hours later, a knock came on the front door. Oscar Braun, all one hundred-thirty-five pounds of him, had "a crow to pick" with his lady neighbor. Mamaw let him in for the Inquisition to begin.

"Now Jaybird, I am no man of trouble, you see. I try bein' a good neighbor all the time and bother no one!" Oscar said.

"Yeah, yeah, Oscar, just spit out what you got to say, or we'll be here all day! I got crops to tend to and these young'un's' will want another meal soon, so speak your piece!" Mamaw insisted.

"We'll, uh, last night somebody went to rockin' my outhouse while I took my daily, uh, well you know! I mean it plumb scared me to death when boulders hit that thing!" Oscar screamed.

Robin, Tim, Phil, and I swiftly decided to find something interesting in the backyard. A football came in handy to toss around.

"So, you got any idea who done it Oscar? You get eyes on anyone?" Mamaw inquired.

"Well, not exactly, but I think I heard laughter out there. I got so mad that I yanked up my drawers and went inside for my pistol; I did!" Oscar answered.

"Land sakes, you old fool! You coulda shot yourself, dummy! And if you're makin' blame this way, remember that bullets ain't got no eyes! Yeah, bullets sure ain't got no eyes, you blind-ass buzzard! If this is all you got to say, well, then there's the door!" Mamaw cursed.

Oscar left hurriedly, mumbling about Willie's ease of speech. Those days were gone forever.

Mom got Mamaw interested in taking Fran out clothes shopping, I suspected, to keep us from getting the third degree. Perhaps if it waited, Mamaw might forget. The ladies left us alone. What a treat!

We boys were busy with three television channels from Knoxville, Tennessee, and Lexington, Kentucky. The local radio waves played bluegrass, gospel, or country, with rock music a rarity. Bored teens were hard to keep in line.

Tim looked at Ms. Carnes's white laundry out to dry on a Saturday morning. He looked at us with a mischievous grin and spoke.

"Boys, y'all wanna have some fun? Mommy hates Old Camelback next door! We got loads of black walnuts piled up near the chicken coop for such an occasion!"

What did we have to lose? If Mamaw hated the old bag, being kin also gave us a reason. Robin stepped back and excused himself. He'd seen Mamaw angry and wanted no part of it. No problem! Three of us were as good as four, anyway!

Phil, Tim, and I gathered armloads of the walnuts and moved into position in three spots out of view. On the count of three, the bombardment began!

Underwear, slips, bras, and t-shirts became easy targets. Man, we laughed silly as Robin hid in the shadows, doubling over in hysteria.

We enjoyed fun and games...for a while. The laundry looked like it had been rolled in black ink, reminding us of the newspaper. We got bored, went inside, and ate a cake baked for Fran's boyfriend. Split four ways, it wasn't half bad, even without frosting. Teens didn't care about ownership, but Fran nearly killed us later!

The ladies returned home. Mom and Mamaw argued over who tried to show the other up more. We played dumb well until the phone rang. Yep, Old Camelback rang to complain about something happening to her laundry.

"Listen Ms. Carnes don't go accusin' my boy of nothin' until you get the facts! And yes, I know how the boy is! I'll get to the bottom of it, for shore! Ain't no way my boy can lie to me, I guarantee that! If I see lies and evil in his eyes, he's finished!" Mamaw wailed.

Phil and I slipped away as Mamaw grabbed Tim by the ear as he got ice water from the fridge. The eruption spilled over instantly.

"Timmy, you messed up that laundry, didn't you? My Lord, I can see it through the winder! Plumb looks to me that a coal heap been dumped on it. Don't try lyin', stupid, I know you done it!" Mamaw screamed as Tim tried pulling away, his fate sealed like a clamshell!

Mamaw beat enthusiastically on Tim as Robin hid in a bedroom! Mom and Fran came out of the room they were examining clothes in. The London circus came to town! Excitement for people of all ages!

Poor Tim leaped, twisted, and shouted to the top of his lungs as Mamaw's four-foot-long garden hose chased him all over the house. Phil and I chuckled outside but knew we were next in line. Mom, the executioner, stood by for her turn.

Fifty-seven swings later, Mamaw caught her breath to determine if Tim had acted alone. Mom yelled out the back door before we got the heat lamp and questioned.

"My two boys better tell me they got *nothing* to do with the laundry next door! You heathens better come in and explain! And I ain't gonna wait all damn day!"

Phil and I made up a quick story, but both fell apart to Mom's face.

"You two little hellions! So, you messed up those clothes! Two dumbbells, I swear! Mom, hand me that hose!" Mom squealed.

Phil and I clubbed into each other as Mom swung wildly on our butts! Robin stayed far away, but I could hear his faint laughter. Some friend, huh?

With several swats getting us both, Mom seemed satisfied. Mamaw wanted her turn, but Mom nixed the idea. We'd been punished enough and never did it again. That plan we shared in Mamaw's presence.

Our next quarterly trip to Kentucky shut out one Robin Welch. He flatly refused to return to the house, which scared the crap out of him. Ironically, the Mamaw stories intrigued little brother Jay Welch to join us instead. How long would it be before our whole neighborhood got in line?

Post Papaw Kentucky
Chapter 10

The mayhem my parents endured on any trip kept this one from being boring. Dad, the persistent speeder, dealt with Mom's attention to his driving with disgust and irritation. The man's depth of love for Mom stayed on display for over four hundred miles.

The arrival at Mamaw's became complicated by Dad's presence and the outlandish stories Phil and I put into Jay Welch's head on our long drive. Dad's disdain for his mother-in-law over her threat to shoot him lingered for years. The warm fuzzies never entirely returned.

Jay Welch lived life as a good sport. His brother Robin warmed him up for the possible haunted house experience he'd seen himself. Jay and Robin were as different as night and day. Jay never intentionally hurt anyone, unlike his bigger brother. A joker with infectious laughter, he fit in with our merry band of idiots. He could not wait to visit London.

The allure of spooky stories to teenagers must be universal. However, with significant effect, my granny laid it on thick to set us up for sleepless nights. I told Jay as much.

"Look, believe what you want, but Robin knows what we saw the night he was so scared. I am just used to weird stuff at Mamaw's, so I wasn't fazed that time."

Jay agreed but wanted the excitement of the paranormal to be taken back as his own. Jay's competition with his older brother modeled mine with Phil. The better the stories for the neighborhood gang, the more status was achieved. Jay needed confirmation that oddities were happening. Mom said Jay and I were sneaky punks, whereas our brothers didn't care to hide it!

After several days without hinting of any spiritual impropriety, we looked for other fun. Mamaw's dog, Tiny, somehow morphed into a zombie canine. He had been younger, friendlier, and intelligent. An accident caused him to meow and not bark. He also lost a patch of facial fur, which gave an unlikely smile. He smelled like a dead dog and got christened "Maggot Mouth" by Tim and our pal Robin Welch. Cruel or not, the label stuck!

One evening, Mamaw made one of Papaw's dishes, goulash, for dinner. We needed to figure out the ingredients. We saw elbow macaroni noodles, beef, tomatoes, carrots, and a deadly dose of lard for good measure. At Mamaw's diner, the options came down to "take it or leave it" at mealtime.

We yearned for Kern's bread from the local bakery whenever we didn't care for the evening meal. Mamaw wasn't shy about buying the day-old versions and keeping them in the deep freeze, as she called it. As with her cornflakes stash, there were always loaves of bread. That night, we didn't get to the toast and Mamaw's homemade butter due to circumstances beyond our control.

Everything went fine as the evening meal progressed. Mamaw allowed us teens to eat in her sacred living room. What a privilege! We needed to behave, but...things happen to teenage boys.

Phil, Jay, Tim, and I carefully carried our dinner plates and sat down together. Our talk about girls, cars, and something lesser enlightened everyone. An appearance by Maggot Mouth himself started an uproar!

Phil spied the poor little dog and quickly covered his nose. We followed suit because the rank odor cut through our steaming hot meal. What happened next nobody can forget.

We were all sickened by the sight and sound of the zombie dog. It bothered Phil the most, as evidenced by his departure from the room. In haste, he returned with my spray bottle of Jovan musk (A 1970s staple!), shook it side to side, and then sprayed it on ol' Tiny- the Maggot Mouth zombie!

I glanced over at Jay to see him gulp in a hearty dose of the air as he tried swallowing milk. Tim and Phil collapsed in laughter, but the good stuff delayed itself about fifteen seconds!

Jay's tipped head spewed milk from his nose like a sieve, and the faucet-like gusher sprayed onto his goulash plate! I instantly burst into such laughter that a head rush caused incredible dizziness, which was fabulous! Tim dumped his plate in his lap, and Phil cackled like the hyena Mom called him! We could not control ourselves!

"Timmy! What you boys doin' out there, carryin' on like jackasses again! Huh? Get to finishin' that meal so's we can start the cleanup. Understand?" Mamaw bellowed.

Nobody stopped laughing long enough to answer our matriarch, and her patience ran out!

"I asked you, Timmy, what in the Hell is goin' on out there! If I get up from here, there'll be four burnin' rear ends when I get through! And when I say something you know durned well that I do it! You'll be twistin' like Chubby Checker if I get up now!" Mamaw screamed.

Poor Tim caught his breath long enough to lie and say he told us an Oscar Braun story that Jay couldn't manage. The uproarious laughter startled the adults, but we didn't care! When everyone calmed down, it meant bedtime.

Poor Tim got the unlucky pick for Phil as his bunkmate in the pseudo barracks at Mamaw's place. Jay and I got the other twin bed across from them. With winter upon us, we settled in for a cold nap under Mamaw's quilts. It didn't last long.

Four teenage boys in a small room meant laughter, jokes, and misadventures. The grownups did not want anything but silence. They failed to recall their own times as teens.

"Boys, I sure got me a hankerin' for that girl from "Dukes of Hazzard," you know, what's-her-name? Man, them short shorts! Whew!" Tim said longingly.

"Now, look, big boy, you better keep those dreams away tonight since I got stuck with your butt here! I am puttin' a pillow between us, cracker! Stay on your side, you punk." Phil said with a laugh that got the room chuckling.

"Phil, now you ain't got to worry none since I am not interested in fellers, not one bit!" Tim said, defending his honor.

"Timmy, we saw "Deliverance" at the drive-in, and it scared us *bad*! That fat guy got caught by those hillbillies and they made him squeal, piggy-like! You say "squeal" in your sleep, and I will *kill* you! Understand?" Phil said as the rest of us laughed, albeit a little nervously.

"Phillip, your imagination is crazy! That's only a movie and that kinda crap don't happen, especially in London! Why if any feller were to look at another 'round here, he'd be swingin' from a tree, wearin' a custom noose! I guarantee it!" Tim said.

Mamaw overheard enough of our conversation to warrant her first and only warning.

"You fellers shut them mouths of yours and get to sleep! I heard enough idle talk for tonight! I can't speak for the rest, but Timmy, if I hear your voice again, you're gonna get an attitude adjustment! And you know what that means! Do I need to remind you, boy?"

We kept our voices down and hoped that the old woman would go to sleep. None of us were too tired, and the vital conversation went on!

"Boys, now you know Oscar's house over yonder is haunted, right? I mean it! Years ago, the old barn had crazy shit goin' on over there! Someone said witches were to blame and everyone stayed away from it. One night a guy busted in on a ceremony and they found him hung up from a rafter a couple days later. The sheriff called it suicide, but we know better! Durn, and his ghost haunts this street every night!" Tim whispered.

Jay and I were not impressed. We both called the story crap and commented as much.

"You mean Oscar's place is haunted and he just lives there like nothing happens? Sure man, sure! Try another one, big boy!" Jay replied with enthusiasm.

"Well, y'all know Oscar can't see two feet in front of his own eyes! How the Hell would he know what's hauntin' him? The man puts the dumb in dumbbell! I'll bet he squats to piss because he can't find his own tally whacker!" Tim said, awakening the laugh button in us all!

"Tim, I done told you I'll plaster yer behind! Here I come, boy! Stupid, stupid young'un!" Mamaw screamed.

Phil, Jay, and I ended up in the same twin bed, struggling to cover any exposed parts to Mamaw's wrath!

Mamaw sliced and diced up Tim's rear end using her handy sawed-off garden hose. Tim tried huddling under the covers, but it didn't work! We heard every swat, holding our laughter so we'd not be next!

"Ouch, Mommy, no! That's killin' me! Stop! I ain't got no place to go here! Cut it out!" Tim pleaded.

The reckoning ended with Tim cussing under his breath. Mamaw might have finished him off if she'd heard what we heard that night!

"Durn crazy woman! Man, it hurts, fellers! Mommy jest don't know when to quit! One of these days they're gonna find her body in the cornfield or in the doggone septic tank! You mark my words! Stupid ol' witch!" Tim muttered.

We hugged our pillows tightly, laughing so hard that we cried into them. Tim could not see the humor in the situation.

"Boys, unless you want me to come over there and body slam you guys, you better hush!" Tim warned.

Phil couldn't resist a crack, considering the conversation.

"Gee, mommy, no! Stop it mommy! Mommy you hit my pecker and its sore! I need an ice pack, mommy! Hahahahaha! Guys, the only fun we get here is watching Tim get his ass beat!" Phil said in his hilarious Southern twang!

Tim got mad and threatened Phil with instant death while Jay and I kept muffled laughter. Another intruder came into the room: Dad!

"You know, your grandmother's already been in once to stripe Timmy's ass and you's guys are askin' for it now, too! And you know she's a windmill in a hurricane once she gets started! Jesus Christopher, you're all idiots. Why do I waste my breath?" Dad said dejectedly and in a whisper.

Dad warned us, so we settled down and drifted off into a sound sleep.

First awake in the morning, I smelled something clearly burning! I sat up and, to my shock, saw Tim clutching his lamp like he'd hold Miss America! The smell came from the lightbulb that burned entirely through the shade. I zipped out of bed and unplugged the lamp, startling Phil but leaving Tim gripping his "woman" as he slept!

Phil rolled off the bed and away from Tim as Jay startled out of his sleep, too! Tim's lips were millimeters from kissing the bulb, and I could not let it happen!

I yanked on the lamp, loosened Tim's grip, and leaned my weight on him as he slumbered. With a hard pull away from him, I put the light back on the bedside table, the burned side facing the wall. Mamaw would roast Tim like country ham when she saw it.

"Gusty, what in the world are you doin' hangin' over my bed? We talked one night about girls, and you get the idea somehow that I'm one? Get away from me, you queer!" Tim said with force.

Everyone else chuckled as I began my defense.

"Look, moron, at the lamp on that table! Just turn it around! Your girl there you almost put a lip lock on! Man, I should have let you get that permanent smile!"

More laughter came about as Tim shook his head over the ruined lampshade. Our fun didn't last long before Mamaw burst into the room.

"Breakfast is ready, young'un's, but you gotta wash them nasty hands before coming to the table! Lord only knows where they been in the night! Hehehehehe!" Mamaw gloated.

We did as commanded before launching into the breakfast buffet Mamaw provided. She never learned anything about "continental breakfast" and wouldn't have changed her style even if she could.

The Dilbert family lived just up the hill from Mamaw's, only a climb over a redwood fence away. They were wonderful people with quirks like everyone else. Sure, they didn't like dirty dishes and proved that by eating from the ice cream container with the same shared spoon. When the scoop came in my direction, I respectfully declined with a hard "no."

When the Dilbert's asked if city folk like Phil and I loved fried chicken for lunch later, it likened itself to asking the Pope if he's Catholic. We propelled over the fence while Tim and Jay lagged someplace.

Oddly, Clod Dilbert opened a garage door, entered a bin, and took out a live chicken! Phil and I stood dumbfounded as the man raised the bird, and with a simple spin, the chicken's head popped off and struck the floor! A fountain of blood spewed from the body as it took off...straight for us!

"Jesus, Gus, it's comin' for us! Dammit, run!" Phil cried.

He didn't have to tell me that as we scaled the fence like special ops troops! Huffing and puffing, we landed in Mamaw's yard as the other guys came toward us.

"Don't do it! That crazy old man Clod just murdered a chicken right in front of us and sent it our direction! Look out, we're goin' inside!" I screamed at my companions.

Tim got the laugh of his life as he climbed the fence to look over the carnage. Jay did an about-face, joining us back inside Mamaw's "safe" house!

Mamaw warned us about breaking her back door down and how expensive they were to replace. We couldn't tell Mom for fear of the "eck, eck" gag reflex from her repertoire. Dad wisely asked her to step out the front door for a word in private.

"Jesus, Mamaw, the guy just rang the chicken's neck, and the thing chased us with no head! I mean, it ran right at us! Clod is a maniac killing birds that way! No, we don't want his fried chicken, that's for sure!" Phil explained.

Mamaw took it all in with Jay standing by her side. Tim entered the house, dying with laughter directed at his nephews.

"Mommy, oh lord, you should have seed them run! I went over the fence where Clod killed the chicken, and he doubled over with laughter! Satan couldn't have made 'em run quicker! I swear! City folk ain't got much for country livin'!" Tim bellowed.

So, everyone got a good laugh at our expense. I pictured that idiotic headless bird catching us both. In my little mind, I surmised I'd punt it like a football into Clod's yard somewhere! What a disgusting trick. Mamaw chimed in, of course.

"Young'un's, jest where do you think fried chicken comes from? You think these durned chickens commit suey-cide or somethin', huh? Ya never found feathers on my table. Hell, no, since I pluck 'em outside! And for your information, we only eat *dumb* animals! Chicken is dumbest of all! You don't see no dogs or cats on anyone's plates, I guarantee that!" Mamaw said with her familiar chuckle.

As usual, none of us could argue with Mamaw's logic. The supreme matriarch let us know it each time we visited.

The 1980s called and promised to be vastly different for Mamaw, Tim, and Fran. The one constant thing in life is change, which comes in abundance.

Hangin' on, Honey!
Chapter 11

Tim missed his big sister every day since she married Hoss near the end of 1979. They got their own place nearby but were out of Mamaw's dominance. Freedom ruled their days, but not so much for my Uncle Tim.

In the Spring of 1980, Mamaw adjusted to cooking for two. Tim, always a hearty eater, got along well with his mother. Usually, that is.

The old rototiller hadn't started for a year when Mamaw commanded Tim to yank it out of her shed and get it going. Her usual crop of corn, beans, potatoes, and anything else she fancied needed soft soil. Tim struggled with cranking the old engine over and the sheer weight of the machine. Mamaw didn't care.

"I said get your dumbass over there, start that tiller and get to plowin', Timmy!" Mamaw screamed.

The half-dead tiller gave out on him each time Tim barely got it moving. The scene repeated itself a half-dozen tries before Tim's patience wore out. Frustrated, he tossed the tiller aside to catch his breath.

"Hey, durn you, get that thing goin' or I'm gonna beat you, Timmy! You hear me? Get a move on!" Mamaw yelled again.

The tired teenage boy walked away in an uncommon act of defiance. Mamaw furiously followed Tim. He picked up the pace each time she got closer until he ran.

Mamaw stopped, knowing she could not keep up.

"Durn you, Timmy Smallwood, I said come back! Get your big ass right back here, boy!" Mamaw insisted.

Thinking he'd run far enough, Tim stopped again to catch his breath but took off again...slowly.

Mamaw's microscopic patience vanished. She bent down and rummaged through the garden dirt, grabbed a rock the size of a baseball, and let it fly. Tim, back turned to his beloved mother, never saw the projectile coming!

Tim tried slowing again when the rock thrown by a seventy-year-old arthritic woman dropped onto his cranium from fifty yards! He fell like a batch of wet cement, laying there when she hovered over him.

"Get up now, doggone you boy! I told you to get up!" Mamaw said, adding kicks into Tim's ribs.

Concussed or not, Tim needed help to his feet to continue the tiller work. He did just that and lived to play another day! Mamaw never exhibited mercy whatsoever.

Mamaw's love for professional wrestling ran deep with her. Although she called it "rasslin," we watched each bout with eyes of wonder. Only Jesus could've pulled her away when it flashed on her TV. One day, while she watched, someone else tried it.

Mamaw's house on a country lane did not prove conducive to pedestrian travel. Nobody with a fully functioning brain walked door to door on her street. One traveling religion lived to regret it.

Mamaw's door was struck by an unseen guest. She heard it but ignored it, concentrating instead on "yeller-head" and the admonition to "get him, kill that boy," at her loudest volume. When the interruption stopped, she opened the door and asked questions.

"Hey now, ain't you the ones sayin' they's only gonna be 144,000 folks in Heaven? Ain't that, right? Mamaw asked.

"Why, yes, ma'am, which is what we teach!" A well-dressed man holding a magazine said to her.

"Well...okay then... I reckon they're already there!" Mamaw said while callously slamming her front door. The people never came back.

Mom needed her Kentucky fix and offered to take me along. While she drove the speed limit in the passing lane from Cleveland to London, fellow drivers provided the "one-finger-salute" as they angrily zipped past us.

As we got close to Mamaw's homestead, I pranked my elderly granny. I wore a red bandana, mirrored sunglasses, cowboy boots, and a jean jacket to compliment my long hair. Gregg Allman couldn't have been prouder of my appearance.

Mom parked the car up the hill out of sight. I walked to the door and knocked. My elderly great-aunt peeked through the curtains and drew back in a rush. She looked like she'd seen a ghost, so she ignored me. I pounded harder, and she opened the door slightly.

"Hey, uh...what do you want, huh?" Aunt Odie asked.

I put out a high-pitched Southern accent and asked to use the phone.

"Hey, now, my car broke down over yonder and I need to use a phone to call a wrecker! Can I use your phone?"

Aunt Odie bluntly said no, but I squeezed my left boot into the doorway so she could not close me out. That's when I heard an awful, unforgettable sound!

I distinctly heard "click-click" as I tried to peer over Aunt Odie's right shoulder. Five feet behind her stood Mamaw with a revolver directly aimed at my idiotic head! I very nearly *pissed* my pants!

I got smart in a hurry, whipping off my sunglasses and bandana. My long hair and bearded face scared the elderly women, but when I spoke up, Mamaw lowered the weapon as Aunt Odie dashed aside.

"Hey, it's me, Mamaw, your favorite grandson! Hey, drop that cannon, please!" I screamed.

Mamaw's beady black-like eyes were squinted as she took a turn to speak.

"Great God almighty, Ode, look at this stupid-ass grandson of mine! Oh, my Lord! Jest look at the hairy-ape face! He looks all the world like a flitter-face if I'd ever seed one! ((Translation: Flitter = vagina) Ode, quick, get me some bloomers so's I can cover his ugly face! Durn you, you stupid, lookin' like a bears *ass*! If I had my druthers, I'd kilt you dead!" Mamaw said, cracking a smile and setting her weapon aside.

Mom pulled the car around and parked it in the driveway. Stumbling out, she laughed herself onto the front porch. Mamaw got irritated again.

"Emily, you *know* this young'un is *tetched*, but now I see who put him up to actin' so stupid! I coulda plumb blowed his head right off! And you, his own momma, sets there up the hill laughing! Y'all ain't got the sense God gave a goose, I tell you! Now you know for sure ain't nobody ever gonna sneak up on Mamaw! She-it no!" My granny said with vigor.

Aunt Odie kept a disgusted look as she shook her head. I asked what her plan was if I had tried to push my way in.

"Honey, oh, you know Jaybird had the pistol! All I had to do was jest step aside!"

Once the commotion settled, my cousin Edith joined us at Mamaw's. Cousin Edith, family caretaker extraordinaire, especially cared for her mother, Aunt Odie. Edith's life of giving should always be exalted. Nobody did it better.

When the rasslin' ended at night, the talk always wandered to the old days. I could not get enough of the tales and wish I'd been smart enough to write them down. I reveled in each story, particularly the gothic horror tales Mamaw specialized in. She provided no shortage of supernatural variety.

"You see, Ode knows what we dealt with back in the holler on the family farm! This woman, a durned witch, we fought tooth and nail for months. Anybody from preachers to the law, heck, even newspaper people could not believe how she tortured us. We chose to leave in the night to escape!" Mamaw crowed.

"Yeah, she'd been evil to us all! Aunt Odie replied. She shore got lucky that Ma and Pa were not violent people. The whole family wanted to dose that ol' witch with gasoline and set her afire! Me and Jaybird kept our own plans fer her, didn't we?"

The air vanished from the room as Mamaw's steely stare drove deep inside her baby sister's soul. I thought immediately of Mafia movies and how folks get silenced. Mamaw spat snuff into her empty vegetable can, sat taller in her chair, and spoke up.

"To me, our family was *too* soft on that ol' witch! We'd taken years to find the perfect homestead and she aimed to push us away. No way did we cotton to that kinda treatment, but...our folks said they'd seen enough! And Ode, you done said enough, dear sister. Enough." Mamaw said, her voice trailing off as her head lifted skyward.

Mom, never keen on scary tales, watched Edith give an okay.

"Jaybird, what about that crazy ol' empty house with the organ playin' at night?" Cousin Edith inquired.

"Well, and Ode knows this one, too. An old house set up on a hill. Hadn't anyone lived in it for years? A gang of us passed the place comin' home late one night after visitin' kinfolk. As we rounded the bend, laughin', and carryin' on like young'un's do, Ev made us stop. She said, 'Listen, y'all hear music playin'?' Sure enough, we all heard it! Why that ol' place had only walls standin', but boy, we ran once we got closer! Ain't nobody wanted to be last since we were feared the boogeyman would grab us! Jesus, we ran like the wind!" Mamaw said, laughing as she recalled the incident.

Mom sat beside me with an upturned nose and grimace. Her skepticism bubbled over.

"Mom, why in the Hell do you gotta tell this stuff so close to bedtime? I've heard these my whole life and I still don't know what to believe!"

An insulted granny did not let the comment pass.

"Little lady, when I tell you these things, you better believe 'em! There are things in this world that no man can explain! There are old haints hangin' round that we cannot see, but they're *here*! You tryin' to make me out a liar, are you?"

Mom played defense, backpedaling and suggesting we all get to sleep.

Although they lived nearby, Aunt Odie and Cousin Edith spent the night. They were excited to see us, and we loved having them stay. A win-win for everybody, but Mamaw put deviant plans into play.

After an evening of wild stories, ghostly encounters, and banter, I crawled into bed and tried to relax. Mom always shared Mamaw's bed, and I never knew why. Mamaw kept a loaded revolver under her pillow, and being prone to nightmares meant a combination I worried about. A shootout in a featherbed could only happen to my family.

Aunt Odie and her daughter Edith went for a back bedroom recently vacated by Tim's visit to Fran's place. (In hindsight, I should have followed him.) They settled in but wouldn't stay that way for long.

I used the bathroom at the back of the house and saw Mamaw in the kitchen. She stood with her right hand in the freezer. She put her left over her mouth to keep me from speaking. I returned to the kitchen as she removed her frozen hand.

"Lordy, don't you say nary a word! Mamaw whispered, "I am gonna show them two what an old haint can do!"

A spry elderly woman, she slumped to her knees and crawled toward Odie and Edith's room. I stumbled into the living room, sat down, and waited.

Minutes went by with no excitement. As I stood up to get back into bed, chaos broke out!

"Mom...mommy, Jesus, somethin's got a hold to me! Dear Lord, it's an old haint, I swear, Jaybird's not kiddin'!" Edith screamed.

My mother scrambled out of bed to greet me in the hallway. I cautioned her about running into trouble.

"What, what you say? Lordy, Jesus, I am gettin' outta here, Edith! This place is haunted for shore!" Aunt Odie screamed to her daughter as her skinny hide hit the floor.

Then, we heard Mamaw laugh at the top of her lungs! She screeched, clapped her hands, and stomped while Mom and I pressed into the victim's bedroom. They were not amused.

"Durn you, durn you, my heathen sister!" Aunt Odie screamed.

"I'll be durned, for shore, that a ghost or ghoul got me! Man, the coldest durned hand touched my foot and I come right outta that bed!" Edith crowed.

Mom giggled, and I fell over a chair while having the time of my life! Mamaw, the joker struck again! Her reputation stood for posterity.

"I almost give myself away there! I heard you two talkin' and I nearly laughed at the foot of your bed. I tried bein' the old haint and I reckon it worked! You two sounded like you'd run plumb through the walls to get away!" Mamaw said between snickers.

It took a while for the cussing to stop as everyone settled down. I felt targeted next, so I stayed guarded when Mamaw's nightmares took center stage.

I heard a distinctly male voice coming from Mamaw's room in the middle of the night. It startled me because, as far as I knew, only one male inhabited the house: me! Did Beelzebub make a return appearance?

The voice came and went, so I walked warily towards Mamaw's bedroom. Thoroughly frightened, I knew pistols, shotguns, and possibly the Father of Lies awaited me. Regardless, I investigated.

I moved slowly and steadily, wondering why this possible demonic voice hadn't awakened my mother. I hunkered down near the end of the bed, not wanting to wake anyone to send me into sudden death.

The voices stopped as I crouched nearby. Hell arrived, and I interrupted! I withdrew back to my room slowly as my heart raced.

Then, the deep, male voices started again when I settled into bed. I knew no living soul invaded the space with my mother and grandmother, so I lay awake for hours. Haunted house? Demonic possession? I wanted answers in the morning!

I awoke to the usual country breakfast fit for royalty. The smells, laughter, and family banter were a welcome sight. I grabbed a plate and sat down.

"Okay, who were you talking to last night, ol' lady?" I asked Mamaw.

"First off, grandson, you refer to me that way again and you'll need some dental work! Mamaw cried. I wasn't talking to nary a soul last night, stupid ass!"

Mom looked at me suspiciously as I told the table the tale from the night before. Nobody believed me, but I know what I heard.

"Oh yeah, you jest were waitin' on that boogeyman that visited these other two!" Mamaw said as she laughed.

This happened more than once. It remains a mystery, but I know it was *certainly* otherworldly.

After Nikki and I married, we lived in Dayton when discharged from the Air Force. The two-hundred-mile drive to Mamaw's conveniently put us there frequently. We spent time with Fran, her husband Hoss, and her son Ronnie Lee. Tim met Sheila, and they were married before long. When my kids came along, they got a kick out of visiting the funniest old lady in America!

We pounded on Mamaw's front door on a Saturday morning. An odd smell came from the house. She opened the door, hugged everyone, and let us in. My nose detected something that smelled like wet, burnt dog hair- very foul!

"Young'un's, now you got here just in time for lunch! I been makin' up a batch of fatback and hog jowls for everyone! Everybody to the table!" Mamaw ordered.

My kids looked around with panic in their eyes! They wanted to run out the door, and I did not blame them. I thought quickly on my feet and announced an alternative!

"Mamaw, I've been promising the kids we'd go out for pizza, and I don't want to disappoint them! Your offer sounds good, but you know, every kid loves pizza!"

"You people don't know good food when it sits right in front of you! I hate to have you come here and not eat. You go spendin' money when you ain't gotta. I reckon I'll get dressed and go with you though." Mamaw answered.

All my kids were relieved and thankful. I could have gotten Father of the Year awards right there. We enjoyed our meal and returned to Mamaw's home with nobody complaining.

At this point in her life, Mamaw put out an acre-sized garden, as she called it. She rounded up three or four fat dogs she kept company. Most were friendly and gentle. One called Fluffy gave us a different story altogether.

Aunt Odie called to say that Cousin Edith would drop her off. A kind soul, she constantly stirred the crowds with Mamaw as her big sister. Her recollections of the past supplemented Mamaw's, even enhancing them.

As dinner hour approached, Mamaw took to the garden to bring in the day's new cache of vegetables. The kids and I sat in the living room with Aunt Odie as she marveled at their growth.

As Aunt Odie got up to find her cigarettes and lighter, one dog took note, and he did not like what he saw. As my elderly great-aunt sauntered her eighty-pound body across the living room, Fluffy attacked!

The rotten animal, with a snaggle-tooth smile, cocked his head sideways. Then he bit Aunt Odie's toothpick-thin left leg like an imaginary corn cob! He started at her ankle, biting upwards rapidly. Blood poured through her white stockings when I punted the little monster into the kitchen!

My great-aunt stepped backward as blood ran into her shoes. By this time, Mamaw came inside to calm the commotion of her yelping dog.

"What *the* Hell is goin' on in here? Why is Fluffy actin' like he's losin' his doggone mind?" Mamaw asked.

"This dog, he, uh, Jaybird, he bit my whole durn leg and man alive, it hurts like Hell!" Aunt Odie screamed.

Before I said a word, Mamaw pounced on the dog like white on rice! She grabbed him around his neck, dragged him across the kitchen floor, and taught him to fly out the back door! Mamaw fumed!

"Ode, I am so sorry! He's never done anything like that before and I bet you he thinks twice 'fore doin' it again! Let me look at those gashes!" Mamaw commanded.

In Mamaw's house, medicine's description fell between medieval and ancient mysticism. The extent of cleaning wounds came from household bleach and/or rubbing alcohol. Mamaw's rules said treatment *burned* to prevent infection! Wounds were cauterized with needles burned on the kitchen stove and applied directly to the skin. Doctors were expensive and could not do any more than she could!

When Mamaw assisted in fixing the wounds, Aunt Odie looked pale. My kids were kept out of sight as Mamaw did her Granny Clampett imitation in the makeshift operating room, AKA the bathroom. My medical assistance meant passing the gauze and rubbing alcohol. Aunt Odie, the trooper, let her big sister operate with little more than a whimper. Nobody doubted her toughness!

Mamaw slowly began to change as time went on. She spoke of herself in the third person with statements like "Mamaw loves you, honey!" She also started the process of "dying" each time she talked with Mom on the phone. My calls were frequent, and I didn't get the death watch guilt trip because Mamaw knew I kept busy with a family of my own. She believed Mom's responsibility meant moving to Kentucky ASAP. Dad wouldn't hear of it.

Throughout the 1990s, I ventured to London each chance I got. We'd take Mamaw to Flea Land, the Sale Barn, Cumberland Falls, or any place her heart desired. We all loved spending time with her. The people at Flea Land didn't share our feelings.

Flea Land sold miscellaneous items of everything imaginable. Each stand or booth sold exciting things to the public. Mamaw challenged them to prove they weren't pawning junk to unsuspecting souls and clearly told them to their faces. One fine salesman of cast iron skillets got an earful as she perused the quality.

"Hey, you, this pan been seasoned yet, huh? I mean, ain't nobody gonna be able to use it if it ain't! Jesus, I mean, every durn thing will stick to it like glue! She-it!" Mamaw said.

The salesman assured her he sold ready-to-use cookware. She didn't believe him and told him so plainly. He clearly sold junk! The old man waved his hands at her and marched away, swearing as he went.

Not partial to rip-offs, Mamaw set out to the next stand to ridicule. When she'd insulted enough, I took her home.

Tim came over after we arrived from Flea Land. His demeanor and sense of fun made him a favorite of my family. Unfortunately, soon after arrival, he stepped on a landmine- politics!

When Tim espoused the virtues of a Republican running for president, I saw Mamaw squint and prepare a rebuttal. I listened respectfully, not wanting to get into the subject and feeling cornered. Mamaw grabbed the whole enchilada with both hands!

"Timmy, I would not hit a dog in the ass with a Republican! She-it, you so stupid! Don't you know these same people started the durned Dee-pression, you dumbass? Here you are a man with education and a respectable job, too! But you walk in here big as a boxcar, tellin' me how to vote!" Mamaw yelled.

Tim shook his head, stared at me, and realized his mama could not be swayed. The political discussion was tabled for another day, decade, or lifetime.

Tim stuck around only a brief time after. Mamaw let him leave while raging about politics for an hour. Her favorite show, rasslin', prepped its broadcast. Oh boy.

Surprisingly, she'd gotten cable TV and landed the remote on Music Television! What? Then she filled me in on a secret.

"Young'un's, I watch this show with the biggest durned e-dits on TV! These fellers are fools, especially the midget they got on here! I swear you'll die laughin'! The show is called "Jackass" and my Lord, they give it the right name!"

So here I sat with my ninety-year-old grandma putting on a show I didn't allow my kids to watch. It seemed a step above the wrestling she adored, but only a little. In her house, her rules prevailed. What happened in London stayed in London!

We went home, but I wondered how long Mamaw could stay in the house by herself. Reports of running water being left on for hours alarmed everyone. She left food on the stove and only shut it off when things were thoroughly burnt and the house engulfed in smoke.

After Dad passed, Mamaw stayed alone in her London home until 2005. She'd always vowed to leave her home "feet first" only and that no one could make her go! Suppose only someone left her a loaded pistol and a comfortable seat on the nearest mountain. In that case, Mamaw promised to finish her journey alone. When she arrived, she pledged to take over Hell, and none of us doubted her intent!

Hell waited. Mamaw needed family, and Mom couldn't wait to get her companionship. All of Eastlake, Ohio, should have been warned. A southern storm brewed and headed up Interstate seventy-one.

Beautiful Ohio II
Chapter 12

When spring 2005 arrived, Mom became lonelier than at any point in life. She sold the homestead and downsized after Dad passed away the prior year. Why she longed for her mother, her archenemy many times, will never be understood this side of eternity. The pair fought like Hatfield's and McCoy's, on the phone, in person, or through the US Mail. To quote my kid brother, "Gus, this is gonna be *fun*! You wait!"

Daily fireworks occurred when my Uncle Tim settled Mamaw in at Mom's new place. This southern hoedown, throw-down, and festival rolled into one nightmare. My intuitive brother Phil thought we should stand outside and sell tickets.

My mom needed a screen door replacement right away. I promised to buy it and install it with Phil's help. Even two chuckleheads like us could figure out removing and changing out a damaged door without much fuss.

My darling Nikki waited with Mom and Mamaw, thereby "taking one for the team," as I reminded her before leaving. While we'd been gone briefly, United Nations peacekeepers should have arrived but could not have gotten there quickly enough. The Mom and Mamaw war resumed as soon as we left.

Upon our return, I backed my truck down Mom's driveway. To my surprise, my irritated bride stood outside, shaking her pretty head. She stomped towards me with a greeting I did not expect.

"Don't you ever, ever leave me alone with those two again buddy! These women are freaking crazy, you know that. You will not believe how they spoke to each other!" Nikki said.

Phil laughed until he cried. Then he said he wondered what took her so long to identify the obvious. Yes, genetically insane people were among us. I offered Nikki no defense of my actions.

"These two old women are talking about cutting each other's heads off, crapping down their throats and murdering each other in their sleep! What kind of mother and daughter duo are they? They called each other whores! They sound worse than the Mafia!" Nikki shrieked.

I told her the actions she'd encountered were with us since the dawn of creation. My dad said they'd fought like cats and dogs for eternity; Dysfunction came with a capital "D" in our family, but I freely admit the entertainment value.

As if things weren't strained enough between my mother and grandmother, another poor soul soon appeared on the deck. Mom worked with a church ministry that visited the ill and those with spotty attendance. Mom put a card over her visor, and the "*lucky*" person fell into her lap when the van hit a bump one day. She went to see a man named Russ.

Russ hadn't attended church for months and explained the reasons to Mom. The man weathered four decades as a widower and craved companionship. The pair hit it off right away. Did Dad send Russ to Mom from the Great Beyond? And if he did, could we all be allowed in on the joke? Russ, the patsy, rode into a role many believe he'd honestly regret later. Russ could not have been a more perfect victim of the prank on the horizon.

Mamaw didn't care to be left alone for hours when the two budding lovebirds slipped away. Never a person for tact or shyness, Mamaw let loose with both barrels.

"Emily, you know you ain't got no bin-ness ruinin' that ol' man's life! If he had any doggone brains, he'd get to lookin' at this family and run out screamin', I tell you that much!"

With Mom in her mid-seventies, the idea of a long courtship didn't sound feasible. Her classic rebuttal bubbled over.

"Mom, if it were up to you, I'd married some ol' redneck with a farm and an outhouse back in a durned holler someplace! You ain't happy so you want everyone else to be like you! No way! You couldn't control me way back then and you ain't controllin' me now!" Mom shouted.

Mamaw reloaded and came out firing with fury.

"You little witch, you better watch that mouth of yours or I'll close it for you! You shore got lucky with Gusty, I'll remind you. You figured you'd try out half of Kentucky and Ohio, too, before you got one to keep! She-it, child, you were born man crazy, and I saw it from your birth! Go on, keep chasin' this old man. See if I care!" Mamaw screamed back.

The eternal conflict brewed to perfection a few months later as Mom alerted everyone that she and Russ were headed to the altar. Mom found someone to hang out with, regardless of what my cantankerous granny thought.

The joyful day arrived, and my sister Linda hosted the big show at home. Family and friends numbered about fifty brave souls. We knew the peace breach approached.

I pulled Linda aside to ask how things were going upon my arrival. She gave me an insight that I will never forget.

"You know, all I can see is Dad up there behind those pearly gates, looking down on this and saying, "*Poor bastard*!" as Linda and I broke into hearty laughter, the point well-taken in my brain.

I found Mamaw and got a quick hug. She revealed her displeasure about the upcoming union, but I expected nothing less. As Russ weaved through the crowd, I watched my saintly granny go into action. "Operation Snafu" came into being.

"Russ. Buddy, you got time to go if you leave now! My husband Willie tried warnin' Gusty by tellin' him 'Good luck, good luck' on tamin' this wildcat! You better run off whilst you have the chance! You been warned!" Mamaw confidently chided.

Russ rolled his eyes, looked at me, and asked, "Do you have that Bible stuff you will say today?" He shuffled me away from Mamaw, ignoring her sage advice. I nodded, and the service went off without issue. The newlyweds were thrilled, and the union provided their elderly version of "Three's Company" sitcom fame.

Poor Russ became the "Switzerland" of a demilitarized zone between mother and daughter. He'd watched the bombs fly overhead, unable to stop them. Sometimes, they came up short and ended up on him. The man could not win no matter what he did. If he cooked a meal, someone disparaged it. Someone accused him of neglecting his appointed duties if he took solace in the backyard. He needed somewhere to run, being outmanned and outgunned on all sides.

Phil took immense pride in quizzing Mamaw on the most random of subjects. His all-time favorite stirred things up by asking Mamaw if she wanted a hog's head.

It went like this:

"Mamaw, can we get you a hog's head for the freezer, uh, you know, like in the good, old days?" Phil asked while setting the scene to his liking.

"Huh, yeah, well you know that's good eatin' young'un's! We wasted nary an ounce on our hogs! From front to back and side to side, we gobbled it all! No animal on God's green earth can be used up like a durn hog can!" Mamaw said with considerable pride.

Mom got incensed, and her queasy stomach accompanied the "eck...eck...eck" machine-gun-style pre-vomit movements she became known for.

Mamaw always looked innocent yet smiled with Mom out of the room. Phil, ever the instigator, laughed as tears rolled down his cheeks. Naturally, I needed to catch up with my own warnings for Russ.

Russ didn't dig it. He'd get a familiar disgusted look, shake his head, and ramble about our disrespect for Mom's sensitive innards. Then came the mini-sermon. I'd be lying if I said we listened politely.

"You guys know how Emily is with that talk and yet you go on? My, my, I don't know how you do it! To be so spiteful, it's a mystery to me." Poor Russ lamented.

Phil, Mamaw, and I exchanged glances. Someone needed to set the "new guy" straight. Who spoke first? Phil took the bait.

"Russ, come on, man! Mom does this crap just for attention. She grabs a tissue, does her "eck, eck" sounds and runs away! In all the years Gus and I have been around, not once has she ever thrown up. It's an act and it's *hilarious*! Nobody is bein' mean to her! She wants attention and that's how she gets it!" Phil said.

Russ disagreed as Mamaw grinned and nodded. She spoke up, too.

"Russ, you'll learn the truth of how things are around here. You'll not pay attention when she goes to showin' off like she does! You will figure it out, you will! I done raised a child that you don't hardly know yet. When you been around a while, you'll for shore get the gist of Emily's crazy actions! And dammit, I want me a hog's head!"

I added nothing to Russ' frustration. The dude's education slowly evolved about our insane family. Dad's imaginary observation at the wedding rang in my ears. Russ didn't yet understand what he'd acquired. He'd entered a living situation comedy that even came with its own laugh track. It's too bad he could not have censored the language or subject material he'd have accosting his mature ears.

The dysfunction spread one day to the subject of water. Phil and I talked about the value of water intake, especially in the hot months. Mom turned her nose up and plunged into the conversation, uninvited.

"Nobody, Junior, drinks a half-gallon of water each day! I get a sip with medicine, or I get water in my coffee and that's it! You two jackals don't know what the hell yer talkin' about, that much I know!" Mom insisted.

Mamaw grinned while Russ, the Imprisoned, nodded in agreement with Mom. He walked the line and danced to the tune she called.

"Well, young'un's you oughta be durn thankful you get any water runnin' in your house. Hell, we had wells and you pumped hard to get that to come out! Yeah, Emily, you're right, I'd like to see you drink that much water just once! You'd for sure piss like an old milk cow! I swear I'd pay big money to see that! You'd not be able to get to that toilet quick enough, I'll betcha! Hehehehehe!" Mamaw put everyone into hysterics, except Mom, of course.

Phil and I tried to go on about how water affects joints and digestion, but Mom heard enough.

"Enough about the water, alright? I am seventy-seven and I drink coffee, Pepsi, and root beer, not water! Look at Russ settin' there, eighty-five, and I know he drinks no water. You dumbbells can shut it up about this, okay? Shit, right Russ?" Mom said.

Russ perked up, raised his eyebrows, and replied.

"Oh, gee, no, Emily, I hate water! Ya know, there's just no taste to the stuff. And could you blame me for not drinking Lake Erie's finest, huh?"

Everyone laughed again, especially Phil, who could not let the comments pass.

"Gee, Russ, can beat the Germans in World War II, but he can't beat Mom! Hahaha! Jesus, Russ, you are a Prisoner of War here and don't even know it! Mom calls the tune and you're the dancer! You're a super freak, yeah, yer super-freaky! Super freak, super freak! Man, this is hilarious, Gus! Look at the inmate. Hahahaha!"

Mom gave us the death stare as Mamaw jumped in headlong.

"Hey, oh, everyone, Russ waits on us here hand and foot. I'm changin' his name to Steppin' Fetchit, I swear it! Poor feller can't get a word in edge ways with Emily talkin' all the time! He's lucky to take a breath without her permission! He prolly must ask if he can wipe his own ass! Hehehehehe!"

Mom left the room in disgust and anger while we chuckled without her. Russ got philosophical when allowed and took the podium with authority with Mom gone.

"You know, I'd like to live to about a hundred and ten if I still got my noodle, I really say!" Russ crowed.

Before I could speak, Phil looked at Russ with complete disdain and horror.

"Russ, and your noodle is already gone if you want another twenty years with Mom! You're friggin' *crazy*! Look, I know I ain't the brightest bulb on the tree, but damn. What a goof! Gus, do you believe this guy? He's worse off than we all thought! Ain't nobody that lonely! Nah, Dad could not have sent his ass here." Phil boasted.

Russ didn't appreciate the statement, but Mamaw and I laughed silly over the reality of it. Death became Russ' only escape from his sentence.

Russ loved taking his new bride and her mother to brunch on Sundays after church. Mostly pleasant, it occasionally turned into mayhem for the trio.

The instigation between mother and daughter always reared its head in public and in a damning way. Mom hated silence and did anything in her power to end it. She did not care who she offended or caught off guard.

One Sunday, an elderly gent came by, and Mom looked into his soul, seeing something amiss. She put out her arm to halt his exit, asking the man a simple question.

"Hey bud, are you happy today?" Mom asked innocently.

"Uh, what? Oh, happy, yes, sure. Yes, I am happy." The surprised man said.

"Well, then *tell your face*!" Mom yelled out in a childlike giggle.

The guy nodded and moved away quickly for a man his age. Mamaw sat with her mouth agape and couldn't help but get in on the fun.

"Emily, you know, someone's gonna take a sock at you one of these days when you get in their face! My Lord, you don't make no sense! You stupid! You wanna make folks in here run up under the table so nobody sees you with 'em! Russ, you got no brains in yer damn head if you like this kinda crap!"

Russ stared into his coffee, knowing he stood no chance at diplomacy. He shuffled into his seat and knew Hurricane Emily had thrust upon them.

"Mother, you know good and well that *nobody* can shut my mouth! That's just how I am! I talk to everybody, and I don't care who likes my hillbilly ways! And you can like it or lump it, too!" Mom replied in her less-than-discrete manner.

"Well, said Mamaw, I got a right to my hillbilly ways too, but mark my words, somebody you irritate on the wrong day will take your durn head off and hand it back to you, wait and see! Judgment Day is just around the bend, my little lady."

Russ squirmed along in the seat, looking helplessly at the dysfunctional carnage. The restaurant crowd demanded more before the senior citizen sitcom went away.

Another show awaited another day. Russ paid the tab and helped his ladies out the door. The cease-fire lasted briefly.

Mom and Russ rarely got away by themselves. When Mamaw broke her hip at age ninety-six, she got a couple of weeks of recovery in a local nursing home. They could not have been prepared for such an independent soul to arrive.

I visited one Saturday evening to find my favorite senior citizen. At check-in, I only said "Jemima" for the desk nurse to point out her direction.

I walked down the hallway to a communal area with a big-screen television and about fifteen seniors mindlessly watching a game show. The only one missing was my granny. Her wheelchair sat strategically placed near a window.

"Mamaw! Hey, beautiful! How are these people treating you in this jail? How come you haven't escaped yet?" I asked in a loud voice.

Mamaw jumped as I came into view. She smiled and reached for a hug, which I willingly gave her.

"Honey, I don't know how long they plan to keep me in this place, but I wonder 'bout them birds outside. Watch 'em! They just keep flyin' together, goin' from one tree to another, then back again. I sure do wonder what makes 'em do that. Ain't nobody chasin' 'em, either!" Mamaw said.

The birds were a mystery to us both. Leave it to Mamaw to find nature to observe and love wherever she goes. Her thoughts then went to another subject: food!

"Durn, this place ain't got food worth a she-it! There's no taste to anything! It's like they think our tastebuds are *already* dead! Well, mister, mine ain't dead at all! I'd like to see these workers try eatin' this garbage! You couldn't make hog slop outta this crap. I don't believe you'd get a maggot to eat somethin' in this place! It should be agin the law! Old folks gotta have rights!" Mamaw yelled.

Between laughs, I offered to get her something and bootleg it in for her. Fried chicken to the rescue? I'd seen her consume it so dearly that the bones looked like they'd been in a desert for a year and bleached white as snow. The woman wasted no meat of any kind.

"You know, when you get rescued from here, I'll wheel you down to Lake Erie to watch those beautiful sunsets with me!" I told her.

"Yes, I love that big lake, but jest don't you try pushin' me in! We both know your mama would throw me in and push me under if she took a notion! No, I'd never go down there with her! Well, I swear, two might go down, but jest one comes back! Hahaha!" Mamaw said with great laughter.

I didn't argue the point or take sides in the longest-running feud in American history. The dysfunction between my mother and grandmother only went back to 1931.

There were more battles in the Jemima-Emily showdown series. The deep distrust and downright hatred came from a place the rest of us never understood.

Mom's husband Russ, a saint by any standard, stepped up to help Mamaw in her final years. Always one with a sunny disposition and willingness to help, having him around meant so much to the family. Russ did everything, including changing Mamaw's undergarments and such.

"Russ, now dammit, I got some decency left in these old bones, you know that. I cannot look you in the face after what you been doin' that my daughter should be! At least Phillip will run when these clothes come off, and she-it, I don't blame him! Dyin' with a lil dignity would shore be nice!" Mamaw said.

"Jaybird, I know you need help, and I don't mind. Think of me as a nurse or something medical, okay? Emily just, well, you know her weak stomach and all." Russ responded.

"No sir, it ain't the stomach she got that's so weak, it's her dad gummed mind that's the problem! Hellfire, I swear I don't know what I done wrong gettin' her raised! She does only what she takes a notion, too, you believe me! That child minds nobody. She been like that since her first breath on this earth and will be until the Good Lord takes her out! I guarantee it!" Mamaw said with a chuckle.

Naturally, Mamaw could not resist a chance to spice things up by being ornery. More than once, she faked death to terrorize everyone, but especially Mom. Mamaw would cock her head to one side, leave her tongue hanging out, and close her eyes tightly while regulating her breathing. She'd lay still as a stone, hoping someone got close enough for her to *scream* at. Constant high jinks!

The family prepped for Mamaw's upcoming 100th birthday in early 2009. We were confident that the ageless, eternal wonder seamlessly entered her tenth decade. Betting people figured to lose out.

Mamaw's retrospection rose as the weeks grew closer. She reflected on days past and how she wished she'd done better. Everyone tried convincing her of God's eternal grace for repentant sinners. It took Tim's family years to see her grasp hold of Jesus firmly. While she leaned heavily on him, she questioned eternity.

"Man, do I got a lot of kin waitin' on me over yonder, you know that? Mamaw asked me one day. I reckon they're gonna know when I roll in there, right?"

"Oh, just wait! It's gonna be a party like you have never seen! Papaw will be there, your folks and especially Ronnie Lee! Mamaw, we've all done things we are not proud of, but as my co-worker used to say, 'Thank God for Jesus', the only reason we get in. Grace covers it all." I reminded her.

"Well, I figure it's gonna take me a while to apologize to folks I beat Hell out of in my early days! I beat people so bad back then that later, well, I got to feelin' sorry for 'em! I hope the Lord understands. My *temper* and no tolerance for stupidity got the best of me." Mamaw said with a sly grin.

My granny cracked me up as she always did. The tough gal persona she displayed also kept a tender side well hidden. The discussion felt familiar but also like a hunch I did not want to feel. Before I returned home, I kissed her forehead and told her of my great love. The admiration ran miles deep.

I got the call that Mamaw passed away two weeks later. She'd been so lucid and animated up to the end. She'd come so close to reaching the milestone birthday and only missed it by six weeks. Our matriarch, the eternally youthful one and a perpetual life of the party, went to her Beulah Land. Another trip for the Stefanow clan to the Bluegrass State hit us with great force.

Beulah Land
Chapter 13

My trips to Kentucky slowed when Mamaw moved into Mom's Willowick, Ohio, home. Tim and Fran's families kept London in check in my absence. Development and the Interstate 75 raceway/meat grinder squeezed the three-hour jaunt from my Ohio home, adding time to the run. It got more unpleasant every year with traffic problems and construction.

Letting Nikki drive proved beneficial in keeping my rage under control and allowed me to gather my thoughts. I knew the family funeral home in London very well. The little church in the holler called Union United Baptist sat across the road from the cemetery, holding the remains of my loved ones. The place scared me even in daylight as a kid, but it became a comfort as an adult.

I expected Mamaw to leave the world in 1980. To envision her without Papaw for thirty years didn't click in my simple brain. They went together like peanut butter and jelly or, more likely, Batman and the Joker. One without the other made no sense.

Mamaw loved crunching cornflakes for me before adding whole milk to them at breakfast. (The only milk besides buttermilk to her.) Her home always stocked those flakes; sometimes, six unopened boxes were visible above her kitchen sink. The Depression was deeply embedded into her psyche, and the woman stored food like a castaway! Mamaw crafted outstanding handmade quilts. The colorful stitched masterpieces graced many beds in Ohio and Kentucky.

I realized as I aged that Mamaw let me live in her world as a privilege. After the "squirty-gun" trial by fire, I walked a fine line in my speech and actions with her. The reverence I showed her meant more as the years accelerated. If I considered myself the front-runner favorite in the grandchild race, why hadn't I written notes from our conversations? Did Mamaw really know how much I loved her? Her icon status in my life should have been plain to everyone.

Only once did she try to take me from this short life. On a sweltering summer day in the 1970s, I sprinted into the house for a cold drink. I'd have been better off with a warm garden hose spewing the rubbery sulfur and liquid iron mix that passed for spring water.

Mamaw delighted herself in lending a hand to her favorite grandchild seeking liquid refreshment. Her ample supply of tin cups in the cupboard proved helpful as one already sat ready for me. When she pushed it across the table, I took it in a large gulp *ala stooge*!

What happened next seemed surreal. The cup toss allowed the "firewater" to entrap my uvula first! I swear it let out a yelp as the poison soaked it! Coughing, gagging, and spitting occurred at once. I feared I'd drown in the "spirits" invading my throat. As my granny belly laughed, I ran to the sink to evacuate the 'shine.

Snot flowed from my nose, tears rained down my cheeks, and anger emanated from my soul as I knew there'd be no point-to-point retaliation! Mamaw consistently outranked anyone.

"Hehehehehe! Oh, lordy, I ain't seed a face like that in a long time! Yes, it's been maybe since I got Willie drunk on 'shine and then put that perm into his hair- been that long! Lordy, you looked like you got yourself a bite outta the devil's ass! Hahaha!" Mamaw yelled.

I cleaned myself up in the bathroom and poured my water into a new glass afterward. The "Queen of Pranks" struck again!

Pranks aside, she'd been a fantastic granny and well ahead of the times. She could not be intimidated by man nor, beast, or situation. Her view on equality struck me as advanced for her times.

"Now, look, I ain't sayin' a woman's always gotta be in charge of things, but dammit, men have nearly destroyed this whole world how many times now? Huh? Like I used to tell Willie, 'Just 'cuz you got that piece o' skin 'tween them legs don't make you better or smarter than me!' He knew I meant it, too, bud! Can men have young'uns? Hell no, and there'd be a lot less folks on the planet if they could, I guarantee you that! "Mamaw bragged.

Nobody doubted the woman's ability to express herself, and few tried offering a differing viewpoint, regardless of the subject.

She never understood why I grew my hair so long to give it away to girls who needed it worse than I did.

Each time, the cross-examination went this way:

"Young'un you know the Bible's agin men wearin' their hair long. That much I know and read somewhere. I figure you ain't read that in the Good Book! I been told that all my life." Mamaw insisted.

I chose my words carefully each time the touchy subject came up. I fully anticipated a "morphydite-morphydite" chant again. Papaw would have skinned me alive if I'd shown up with hair past the middle of my back or in a "woman's" ponytail style he hated. I produced my comical response.

"Well, you know about Samson, right? You know, the man with long hair as his *strength*! Yeah, he's my favorite Bible character, my dear grandmother!" I said with a confident smirk.

"Good Lord, Gusty, you so dumb! Samson got his durned eyes poked out and died from pullin' a buildin' down on his head! You stupid! What an e-dit! You *tetched*, young'un, and I mean it! Got no sense, I swear! How you wear that durn hair of yours don't make me no never mind! She-it! We gonna go round and round about a subject that don't mean road apples (Translation: horse manure) to me!" Mamaw crowed as I chuckled nervously.

I never tried explaining my convictions or my way of giving back to the broken world to her again. Enough said.

Mamaw regretted extraordinarily little in life, but some things affected her. The pranks and orneriness she laid on her little sister Odie gave her pause in later years. I asked for clarity on her front porch one day.

"Well, you know I was a monster sometimes to my own kid sister Ode. Yeah, I gave her Hell on earth, yes, and her child Edith, too! Haha, my meanness got the best of me! I jest could not help myself when I wanted to be ornery. Somethin' just took over, I reckon!" Mamaw said.

I wanted specifics long before I thought of drafting this book. Why didn't I take detailed notes? I suppose I was too caught up to grab pen and paper. My problem.

"I mean you can scare the crap outta some people and get no hard feelin's, you know? Not only did I do it to my sister, but with her bein' pencil thin, I shoulda considered that but I never did! Hellfire, she coulda been kilt right there before my eyes!" Mamaw said, shaking her head.

I asked about paranormal events at the house on Moren Road. Rumors abounded from the first time anyone set foot in it.

"Dammit, ain't no old haints livin' here in this house! The scariest thing in my house is me and you can take that to the bank, mister! Sure, I know there's scratchin' in the walls at night, but it ain't nothin' but field mice burrowin' in! Your boy Robin Welch, well, he's gone and told all of Cleveland about this place like it's full of spooks and specters! He ain't seed crap here and he knows it! That boy got more bull she-it than a Christmas turkey, I tell ya the truth!"

I kept the demonic voices coming from Mamaw's room under wraps. From what I heard, someone channeled Barry White through her. I kept the conversation light and instead asked about the Netherworld beneath her tub. Surely Satan and his imps lurked below! We couldn't be convinced of anything less.

"Y'all got strong imaginations, that's for sure! There ain't nothin' under that tub but dirt! Why no beast stayed under that place! My daddy always said for us to fear the living, not the dearly departed! Only real, live humans do body harm! Dumbasses, I swear!" Mamaw crowed.

A bear came down from the mountains one year and did not take Mamaw by surprise. Her arsenal of firearms meant she'd defend herself against an army. Tim sent London police officers to the house for a wellness visit. They needed one themselves when Mamaw finished with them.

The police arrived and knocked loudly due to Mamaw's hearing-challenged ears. She came to the door with a loaded shotgun in hand.

"Miss Smallwood, my Lord, please put that weapon down! We're here to see if you're okay. Tim sent us, Miss Smallwood, your son!" Said one worried officer.

"I heard tell of a bear loose 'round here and I absolutely will not let go of this gun! I'll fill his butt full of lead same as I would anyone else's! Ain't no bear gonna eat Mamaw, that you can be guaranteed of! It don't make me no never mind to kill a durn bear! He pokes his head near me, and I'll drop him like a bad habit, I will!" Mamaw screamed.

The police officers returned to their patrol car's safety and told Tim his mother did not comply. Tim showed up moments later and got the same result. Mamaw filled me in on the rest of the story.

"Well, yonder come Timmy big as an ox, tellin' me to put the guns away and stay inside. Hell, I would not be waitin' on no bear to come knockin' at the door. If I seed him near my yard, I'd blast his rear end to kingdom come and I'll have me some bear meat, which I ain't never tried...yet! Hehehehehe!" Mamaw said as she laughed heartily.

These familiar stories of her bravery, honesty, and general orneriness made her an irreplaceable part of the family. Her top-notch storytelling entertained the masses. I wondered how she viewed me through the lens of her tainting me with the *tetched* tag. It felt like she held it over my defective head.

"Well, as young'un's go, you weren't so different than the rest in some ways, I reckon. I beat you only a couple of times. You never went outta your way to get on my nerves as Phillip did. Lord, that child is past *tetched*, and Emily for shore can't see it! But you, now, you couldn't be yer daddy and get away with them wisecracks and pranks! Only *one* Gusty came into this here world. Just one! Junior or not, you had to be who the Good Lord *made* you to be! No matter how my grandkids treated me, I still loved them all. Even the durn mean ones! Phillip, that boy, that child was king of meanness, for shore!" Mamaw said with vigor.

I didn't push my luck and tried to change the subject. Mamaw knew another tale and couldn't wait to blab.

"One year me and Ode came to Cleveland for Christmas time on the Greyhound bus. We planned to stay a couple days so's we could have Christmas Day with our families. We loved the visit until you and Phil got stupid! I mean it, two dummies took to hidin' in our closet! You two could not scare my sister and me. How dumb could you get?" Mamaw said.

"You wouldn't believe the trick we played on you and Aunt Odie. We had you good!" I crowed.

"Oh sure, I knowed and so did Ode! Y'all wanted to see two old women asses, for sure! And you remember what I did? I know you do! I dropped my jammies, put my butt to the closet door as you boys hollered like babies! Hahahaha, Hehehehehe! Ode laughed 'til she cried as you two took off like gallopin' horses- stumble bums! I showed you! You two e-dits learned to never try it again. I can say that about you- you learnt! Ol' Phil, Hellfire, he'll never learn a durned thing! He's the aggravator not seen since the world began! That boy could get a statue to swing at him!" Mamaw said through laughs.

Mamaw's earthly pains came from losing both of her husbands. Johnie Brummett went at such an early age as Mamaw's first love. I thought it a tragedy also that I only knew him by his accident and local headstone. Papaw's death after retirement meant Mamaw's golden years were barren of his companionship.

Mamaw's tragedies struck my heart with an emotional explosion, especially as I thought about Fran's life. First off, dealing with Mamaw as her mother became no picnic. Then, after marrying Hoss and having her son Ronnie Lee, things turned around, temporarily for the better. Then, on December 8th, 1990, I got a three-a.m. call that I assumed meant Mamaw's passing. Instead, a drunk driver killed Ronnie Lee, along with two older cousins. Fran and Mamaw died emotionally that day, and neither fully recovered from the tragedy.

In 2004, a construction supervisor killed Hoss in a mountain accident. Fran got cancer about a year later, beat it, and then relapsed in 2007. She died in early 2008, but Mamaw's doctors warned us not to tell her of the event. Imagine Mamaw's shock upon her own passing. What a reunion!

All these stories flooded into my peanut-sized brain as we went along. Would Mamaw be at the blessed reunion one day? She needed to grasp the Gospel. Tim and Sheila got Mamaw to think about eternity- no easy task. Better late than never.

Mamaw's relationship with her daughter-in-law started off on shaky grounds. For one thing, she never tried to pronounce her name correctly. (To me, it always sounded like Sheol- the Biblical grave/Hell/Hades in Jewish tradition!) For another, taking Tim away meant that Mamaw fended more for herself on the family homestead. Guess who got the blame for that. Mamaw never minced words with anyone, and Sheila knew it well.

What turned the icy heart of a jilted grandmother into warmth and love? Adding a granddaughter turned darkness to light, winter to spring, and permanently caused old wounds to scatter. All universally cheered the outcome.

Tim and Sheila added two more girls to the family, and Mamaw beamed with pride. As the girls learned to read, they shared Bible stories with their granny, who'd given up trying to understand their meaning. Mamaw's inability to change kept grace an abstract concept meant for others and not for her. One day, it all *changed*.

Tim called me, out of breath and praising God loudly! What happened to cause the joy leaching through the phone?

"You are not gonna believe me, but Mommy has done it! She finally understood grace and accepted Jesus as her Lord! She knows she's goin' to Heaven when she leaves here! I cannot get over it. I do think the girls reading their stories and the Bible to her finally hit her in the heart. Can you believe it? My mother finally understands grace!" Tim shouted.

I stared and said nothing. I'd danced around the cause of Christ with my granny many times. She believed that good people get to Heaven and bad ones go to Hell. That was drilled into her head. Regardless, she'd just glare at me, drop her chin so I could see both beady, near-black eyes, and then tell me how *religious* her folks were. I even asked about her foul language just months before she died.

"Mamaw, where'd you get such a filthy mouth? Ma and Pa Smith must've been handy with foul language, right?" I asked, with the subtlety of an uppercut to a glass jaw.

"Oh now, honey, my folks were loving Christian people. They wouldn't cuss if you hit 'em with a shovel!" Mamaw answered.

I laughed as she continued.

"Honey, I reckon I just learnt all the words!" Mamaw yelled!

Did she have any regrets about this life?

"No honey, I jest cannot think that far back anymore. I know it's better to be a "has-been" than a "never-was!" If you got somethin' you wanna do, you better get to it since no man is guaranteed tomorrow and you know, sometimes I beat people so bad that I felt sorry for 'em... much, much later! I don't know why I could not stop myself sometimes." Mamaw insisted.

We went to the London funeral home. Although the day I'd envisioned for decades arrived, it still hit me hard. My Mamaw never failed to tell me that she loved me. I loved her despite her ways, and she died a family *legend*.

I made the rounds to greet grieving families, especially Tim and Sheila. Wang appeared with the "mullet-fish" 1980s haircut he kept in his own style. Cousin Edith stood calmly, ever vigilant, but reflecting on a life well-lived. Tears flowed, but so did the laughter! Wang and I shied from the casket, fearing Mamaw kept one last prank to spring on us!

"Man, uh, you goin' up there, my cousin? I'll go *if* you go with me. You know that old woman put the fear of God in me! You know how she went on with those old haint stories to rile us! I ain't for sure she won't reach up and pull me in!" Wang said with a hint of fear in his shaky voice.

Mamaw, the eternal one, didn't line up with death as the end of her. I accompanied Wang since he expected it. We leaned on each other and expressed deep reverence.

I marveled at how one so seemingly in the enemy's grasp would stand in glory one day, awaiting us all. Incredible! Only the *grace* of God made it happen.

The funeral proved a simple, country affair, with a no-frills celebration of life. The sting of death always hurts, but the newness of life she'd gotten just in time made me eternally thankful.

The procession that took the casket into the waiting grave shined a light on the relatives already in the Great Beyond. Mamaw and Papaw reunited meant everything to the grieving. The Christian hope says we'll see them in a place sometimes called Beulah Land. The lyrics were perfect for the occasion:

"O Beulah Land, sweet Beulah Land,
As on thy highest mount, I stand,
I look away across the sea,
Where mansions are prepared for me,
And view the shining glory shore,
My Heaven, my home forevermore!"
(Public Domain, 1876)
THE END

Also by GUS STEFANOW

She called me TETCHED

Watch for more at https://www.facebook.com/
profile.php?id=100089276174602.

About the Author

Author Gus Stefanow resides in beautiful Ohio. Semi-retired, he keeps busy with grandchildren and supporting his wife's non-profit organization. He writes to inspire using humor, love, and a healthy dose of irreverence. His simple theology is to love God-love people.

Read more at https://www.facebook.com/profile.php?id=100089276174602.

Milton Keynes UK
Ingram Content Group UK Ltd.
UKHW012251290324
440241UK00004B/283